ALL RIGHT ON THE NIGHT

ALL RIGHT
ON THE NIGHT

V. C. CLINTON-BADDELEY

PUTNAM

GREAT RUSSELL STREET LONDON
MCMLIV

FIRST PUBLISHED 1954

MADE IN GREAT BRITAIN AND PRINTED BY
THE CAMELOT PRESS LTD., LONDON AND SOUTHAMPTON

Contents

Illustrations

ILLUSTRATIONS IN THE TEXT

Preface

IN RECENT years a good deal of research has been done on the materials and organization of the Georgian playhouse. We begin to know the facts about such things as the shape of the orchestra, the uses of the stage doors, the structure of the scenery grooves, the geography of the pit passage. We can reconstruct the building; but it is not so easy to fill the place with voices.

These studies, and the pictures that go with them, are concerned with behaviour not materials, with people not bricks and mortar. They are an attempt to peer inside the playhouse, to survey the impotence of managements, the irresponsibility of actors, the tears and the tyranny of audiences—subjects for research quite as important and nearly as obscure as the history of the theatre itself. The uses of the curtain and the management of the candelabra have been the subject of much learned discussion; but I cannot recall any very detailed examination of Georgian playhouse manners.

Individually the various evidences are fairly well known; there is plenty of information about the theatre in the plays, letters, newspapers and biographies of the period. But it is only when these are examined together that the weight of their testimony can be accurately measured. One may have noted the recurrence of tears in the Georgian audience without realizing the full extent of the inundation; one may have recognized their

addiction to conversation, and yet be astonished at their
united uproar; one may have been aware of their capacity
for applause, and yet be amazed by the total of their
enthusiasm. The first five of these chapters are an attempt
to examine these simple manifestations—and, indeed,
so is the sixth, for Mr. Vincent Crummles's Portsmouth
theatre is more alive today than any text-book playhouse.
The chapter on the pantomime is separate from the rest,
but it too is a study in the spirit and the tradition of
the pantomime, not its chronological development,
the facts of which have already been set out by such
writers as Cyril Beaumont, M. Willson Disher and
A. E. Wilson.

Theatre riots have not been included because these
have been widely discussed elsewhere and belong to the
general history of the theatre. The seventh chapter
contains a collection of articles on custom and behaviour
in the Georgian theatre.

In the main my authorities have been printed works,
generally available, and the Burney collection of newspapers; but unpublished records in the British Museum,
and in the Enthoven collection at the Victoria and Albert
Museum, have supplied much of the material for the
articles on "Bones", "Benefit", "Keeping Places", and
"Orders". I have also been able to draw upon unpublished records of the Norwich theatre, kindly com-
municated to me by the late Aubrey Mallalieu, whose
grandfather and great-grandfather, George and James
Smith, were successively managers of the Norwich
circuit. Since Mr. Mallalieu's death these records have
been mislaid. Presumably they were sold with some of
his books and will turn up again in due course.

The Georgian period in the English theatre does not

mean precisely the period of the four Georges. 1714 is too close to the practice of the Restoration stage, and 1830 means nothing at all as a boundary in theatrical history. Any dates will be arbitrary, but 1737 and 1843 have much to recommend them—1737, the year of the Licensing Act, which confined the drama within fixed limits, and 1843, the year of the Theatres Act, which liberated the stage from regulations which had long ceased to make sense. 1843 certainly marks the beginning of the end of the Georgian period in London (in the provinces Georgian manners lingered longer), and for a start 1737 will serve: these studies will not often stray outside those limits.

The lack of discipline and organization in the Georgian theatre seems very strange in these days. But until quite recently there were relics of Georgian manners among us, which were hardly noticed for extraordinary when they were employed by ourselves.

In one of those mushroom London play societies I have known what it was to be paid by shares in the twentieth century, and to receive as a result a shilling or two for a week's work. In the same society I remember a well-known but ancient actor who had the impudence to read his part from a book. On tour with Ben Greet, I made my first appearance on the professional stage in a leading part; I remember a matinée being dismissed because there were only three people in the house; and the appearance of a star actress "for one night only", displacing for that performance the ordinary member of the company. I remember amateur actors playing small parts in a professional repertory company, in support of a large Shakespearean production; and, strangest of all, an amateur actor being urgently called to play a part

in a London theatre when a principal fell ill and the
management had provided no understudy.*

I witnessed these curious things (all typical of behaviour in the Georgian theatre) between 1922 and 1932
—before Equity arose to knock the last nail in the coffin
of Georgian irresponsibility.

THE PICTURES

The four pictures by Thomas Rowlandson are reproduced from water-colour drawings in the collection of
Mr. Gilbert Davis. The first shows Mrs. Siddons, rehearsing with old Kemble and Henderson. The great
mirror in the background makes it fairly certain that they
are working in the green-room. Henderson holds a
manuscript, old Kemble a printed book—which, together with his attitude, suggests that he was coaching
his daughter and not performing with her. (Page 32.)

"Actors Rehearsing" shows the stage of what looks
like a provincial theatre of no great importance. It is
drawn from the back, looking towards the curtain. The
fact that most of the characters are in costume indicates a
rehearsal called shortly before performance—doubtless
for the benefit of the gentleman in ordinary dress, who
still holds his lines and is evidently appearing at short
notice. The variety of costumes, from Cavalier to Roman,
would not be unlikely in a long mixed bill. The picture
is not more remarkable than the green-room scene in
Nicholas Nickleby, with Mrs. Crummles in full regal

---

* This was in 1927 at the St. Martin's Theatre during the run of *Behind
the Beyond*. Mr. Roland Culver's part was taken for several performances by
Mr. Prescott Hedley, who had played the part a few weeks earlier in the
Cambridge A.D.C.

costume, Miss Snevellicci in tights, and Mr. Folair, as the savage, sharing a pot of porter with a demon.

The lady in the top right corner, and the pantomime beast with the regretable manners, are standing on the ladder leading to the box and window over the proscenium door. The direction of the ladder may, or may not, be one of Rowlandson's mistakes. One would have expected it to lean the other way. (Page 33.)

The picture called "The Prologue" provides excellent evidence of the intimacy which existed between actor and audience in the Georgian theatre—especially in a small theatre like this, a country theatre, one would suppose, from the small depth of the boxes. This drawing was certainly not made in the theatre. It is a sketch from memory and contains a number of inaccuracies. The footlights have been left out; the grill under the stage box is at right angles to, instead of parallel with, the front of the stage; and the orchestra is crowded beyond possibility. Some joke in the prologue presumably accounts for the faces peering through the curtain. (Page 49.)

The last of the Rowlandson pictures was published in 1807 over the caption, *"Miseries of Public Places.* After the play, on a raw, wet night, with a party of ladies fretting and freezing in the outer lobbies and at the street doors of the theatre, among chairmen, barrow-women, yelling link boys, and other human refuse, in endless attempts to find out your servant or carriage, which, when found at last, cannot be drawn up nearer than a furlong from the door." (Page 145.)

The picture by Robert Dighton, "At a Tragedy," (? 1797) is taken from a mezzotint (coloured impression) at the British Museum. This, and its companion picture, "At a Comedy," are less well known than the similar caricatures by Rowlandson and Hogarth. Another comment on the same theme is the cartoon by Isaac Robert Cruikshank of a dandy having the vapours in a box at the opera (1818). It is reproduced from an etching in the British Museum. (Page 64.)

The George Cruikshank pictures of "The Stage Assassin" and "The Stage Prince" are reproduced from *George Cruikshank's Table Book* (1845). These woodcuts originally accompanied burlesque articles by Gilbert A'Beckett, and are included here because they so vividly suggest the theatre of Mr. Vincent Crummles. The Prince is in the act of throwing aside an entirely inadequate disguise, to the delight of his loyal subjects, and the confusion of the usurper and his supporters. (Page 110.)

The last George Cruikshank picture, an etching from *The Memoirs of Joseph Grimaldi* (1838), is not reproduced for the sake of the great clown at his farewell performance in 1828, but because it shows spectators standing in the wings of Drury Lane, 'between the scenes', in full view of the audience. The picture also shows a stage-box and the proscenium door and window. (Page 160.)

Other views of the stage boxes and proscenium door are afforded in the Rowlandson picture, "The Prologue", and, on the grand scale, in the delightful and little known water-colour painting by Eugène Louis Lami from the Enthoven Collection at the Victoria and Albert Museum. The picture shows Rachel on the stage of Her Majesty's Theatre at the close of the season of 1841. Notice the number of top-hats at hand for waving. Much later than 1841 the waving of hats and handkerchiefs was still the accepted way of acclaiming Irving's first and last nights at the Lyceum. (Page 48.)

The two pictures by Theodore Lane (1800-1828) are

reproduced from a series of six coloured engravings in the Enthoven Collection. "Contending for a Seat" shows the top-hats which men at that date were prepared to wear inside the theatre. "Never sit in the boxes of a theatre with your *hat on*," the author of an etiquette book thought necessary to remark as late as 1834. "It is an insult to the rest of the audience especially if there be ladies." Even then the writer was not prepared to correct the manners of anyone outside the boxes. The picture also gives a good view of the pit benches. Backs to the benches were a late comfort. The Haymarket did not get them till 1843, the Lyceum not till 1878. Pit benches with backs are shown in Phiz's theatre picture in *Bleak House* (1853). (Page 144.)

"Taken Places Occupied" offers valuable evidence on the subject of booking seats at the beginning of the nineteenth century. The man with the watch in his hand, and the smug smile, plainly indicates that a seat could only be reserved up to a certain time. (Page 209.)

An astonishing example of the 'breeches part' is the portrait of Louisa Nesbitt, as she appeared with beard and moustache, in a revival of Mrs. Behn's play, *The Young King*, at the Haymarket in 1837. This is taken from a coloured lithograph by J. Deffett Francis in the Raymond Mander and Joe Mitchenson Theatre Collection. (Page 161.)

The Drury Lane Tally Sheet (1816) is one of a large number in the Enthoven Collection. These papers are extremely interesting for their demonstration of the traffic in free seats. According to this sheet, 133 were free in the sense of being subscription seats or 'free privilege'—but, on top of that, 378 orders were issued for the boxes, 111 for the pit, 182 for the gallery: there were 75 newspaper seats, 65 bones, and 60 actors' tickets in the boxes and 60 in the gallery. Altogether there were 922 non-paying seats, not counting the 133 officially free. One is not surprised to find that the takings were only £65 16 6. (See also pages 156f, 188f.) (Page 208.)

The illustration of pantomime masks is reproduced from an engraving by Alfred Crowquill in *The Illustrated London News* (December 29, 1849) of *Harlequin and Good Queen Bess* at Drury Lane. There are many good pictures of pantomime masks in the early issues of that magazine.

The last plate, from *The Illustrated London News* of January 3, 1863, shows two pictures from the great days of spectacular scenery. The lower picture represents "The Haunt of the Wood Nymphs", a scene from the opening of the Drury Lane pantomime *Goody Two Shoes* by E. L. Blanchard. The other shows the climax of the transformation scene in Henry J. Byron's *Harlequin Beauty and the Beast* at Covent Garden. "It presents," wrote the theatre critic, "the strong contrasts of moonlight and sunshine, and the result of the combination is perfectly delicious." (Page 225.)

For allowing me to reproduce pictures in their collections my thanks are due to Mr. Gilbert Davis ; the Keeper of the Prints at the British Museum; the Keeper of the Prints at the Victoria and Albert Museum; and to Mr. Raymond Mander and Mr. Joe Mitchenson. I am also very grateful to Mr. G. W. Nash for his help at the Enthoven Collection; to Mr. Laurence Irving for information about Lyceum benefits; and to Mr. Richard Southern for kindly discussing with me the architectural details of the Rowlandson pictures.

V. C. C-B.

I

ALL RIGHT ON THE NIGHT

"I have heard, from a very clever person too, that in rehearsing a tragedy, there is not the slightest occasion to speak in a dismal voice, or to put on a long melancholy face, so long as you assume it at night."

Edward Fitzball, Thirty-five Years of a Dramatic Author's Life, 1859, vol. 2, p. 293

"I am resolved to go no more to see the first time of acting, for they were all of them out more or less."

Samuel Pepys, March 1, 1661–2

B

I

THEATRICAL enthusiasts regard the eighteenth and early nineteenth centuries as the Golden Age. Those were the days when actors could claim to have been born in the dressing-room, and to have appeared on the stage in long clothes. Even as children they were a race apart, playing their games in an unexpected world of sliding forests and disappearing mountains, of clouds and collonades and castles, and cottages embowered in preternatural blossom.

One does not think of the modern actor as a member of any such peculiar and mysterious society. He is not constantly concerned with some new theatrical labour, constantly on the road, constantly mugging up new parts or fussing about properties and costumes. He is less often in work than his predecessor, and when he is in work he does not have to worry about the same things: moreover he may play the same part for a year and a half, and that gives him leisure to develop other interests.

The romantic age of the theatre is over. It is no longer possible to tell an actor at fifty yards by the cut of his clothes and the calculated mannerism of his walk. But those artists of the past, proudly professional and reared in the theatrical hamper as they were, were also, in a curious kind of a way, profoundly amateurish. This modern age of theatrical discipline can hardly comprehend the extraordinary lack of organization in the eighteenth-century theatre.

A beau thought nothing of climbing on to the stage and interrupting the play in order to fulfil some silly bet; the actors and actresses thought nothing of interrupting their own performance in order to appeal to the audience in the settlement of some silly quarrel; and the audience thought nothing of interrupting the actors in order to exact an apology from some player who had offended them.

A manager often had to crave permission of the audience to substitute another play for the one advertised; or sometimes a different cast was announced at the last moment. Actresses, particularly Mrs. Abington, often refused to appear for purely capricious reasons. "Sure there never was such an infernal woman as Mrs. Abington", wrote Thomas King to Garrick. And, Garrick wrote to her, January 28, 1775: "You mention *your great fatigue*. What is the stage come to, if I must constantly hear of your *hard labour*, when from the beginning of the season to this time you have not played more than twice a week!" On October 29 of the same year he was writing to Mr. Yates about Mrs. Yates: "She played but thirty times last season, and as she goes on, in the proportion of four times in six weeks, she will play twenty times in this season. Indeed, Mr. Yates, this will not do, and I give you fair warning."[1]

As for "Laugh, clown, laugh", and the notion that a player must sacrifice his own feelings in order to keep faith with the public, such ideas found very little accommodation in the hearts of the Georgian actors. Within four pages of Genest's account of the Bath season 1822–3 it is recorded, first, that Miss Carr had been rendered "utterly incapable" by the loss of a parent, and was unable to appear, and, second, that "Liston was to have played, but was prevented by the death of a relation." "The curtain must go up", a firm article of theatrical faith today, seems originally to have been a supplication from the management rather than a rule of conduct with the players. George Frederick Cooke was frequently absent from the theatre when he was advertised to play, and frequently did play when he was too drunk to speak.

When Garrick and Peg Woffington were playing in Dublin—Lear sleeping with his head in Cordelia's lap —a gentleman stepped upon the stage and threw his arms around Mrs. Woffington's neck.[2] When Mrs. Siddons was playing Lady Macbeth at Leeds in 1799, the call-boy, who had gone to fetch her a can of ale, marched on to the stage and attempted to deliver it during the sleep-walking scene.[3] When Mrs. Jordan was scoring her first successes in the provinces, jealous rivals used to gather in the wings in an attempt to disconcert her; and, later, Mrs. Jordan stood in the wings herself to disconcert Mrs. Robinson.[4]

Mrs. Clive used to glance from the stage to recognize her great acquaintance in the boxes. Now and then she would drop them a curtsy.

In the modern theatre the powerful lighting acts as a barrier between actor and audience. In the milder illumination of the Georgian play-house it was easier to see the audience and therefore more difficult to avoid noticing them. But Georgian celebrities were not obliged to make such a social ceremony of their appearances. A popular singer would behave as though he were conducting a levée. Pacchierotti "found me out and gave me several smiles during the performance", reported Miss Burney with evident pleasure (November 20, 1782); "indeed, he could never look either to the right or left without a necessity of making some sort of acknowledgment in return to the perpetual bows made him from almost every box in the house."[5]

Of all the unprofessional practices of the Georgian theatre the worst was that of introducing popular or moneyed amateurs to try their luck in important parts. When *Eurydice* was played at Canterbury in 1732 there were "several Dances between the Acts by Gentlemen of this City for their own Diversion." In 1748, at Canterbury, Hamlet, the Ghost and Horatio were all played by local gentlemen; and in 1763 an amateur played Falstaff and Boniface. The ladies also insisted on diverting themselves. A gentlewoman played Lady Townly at Maidstone in 1753, and at Richmond several young ladies appeared for the first time on any stage, unabashed, it seems, by such frighteningly difficult parts as Polly and Mrs. Sullen.[6]

These mysteries are not hard to interpret. No doubt the ladies and gentlemen paid for their privilege. They also attracted patronage. And so the eccentric Lord Barrymore was allowed to play Harlequin at the Brighton theatre,[7] and Scaramouch at Richmond;[8] and even Tate Wilkinson permitted a local nob to act Pierre in *Venice Preserv'd* at Doncaster.[9] Ryley records the delight of some country barn-stormers when "some spirited gentlemen, beholding our fruitless struggles, proposed to perform Archer, Aimwell, and Boniface, in *The Beaux' Stratagem*, and the reason is contained in his following sentence: "This of course brought a good house."[10]

Country players were fighting against starvation. London managements were not. Yet exactly the same crafty considerations prevailed with them. Thomas King told Ryley that, failing talent, "patronage is necessary; I have known a person much beneath mediocrity, when introduced by nobility, draw a crowded house. . . ."[11] In December 1800, George Frederick Cooke, in his first triumphant season at Covent Garden, acted Iago to the Othello of "a Medical Gentleman of very respectable connections and considerable literary talents", whose characterization was described by *The Times* as "shapeless and miserable . . . the exhibition never surpassed and was frequently below mediocrity." Two years later (as Boaden reports, without censure or critical comment) "A Mr. Foot, a Winchester scholar, and by profession a printer, attempted Hamlet at Drury Lane"; and, "A Mr. Turner, the barrister, who attempted Macbeth at Covent Garden theatre, now much improved, played Richard III at Drury Lane; he even repeated the character."[12] In 1815 one Edwards appeared as Richard at Covent Garden, and drew upon himself, and upon the managers, the indelible obloquy of a review by Hazlitt.

In Georgian London the stage-struck did not waste their time gaping at celebrities and collecting autographs. They joined "spouting clubs", where the members regaled each other by rehearsing scenes and passages from favourite plays;[13] and those who could afford it paid good money to be allowed to play a part in a real theatre. Charles Mathews paid ten guineas for the privilege of appearing at the Richmond theatre, and Pierce Egan describes a whole cast who paid various prices to appear in a performance of *Othello* at the Haymarket. Many years later, on August 11, 1856, Henry Irving paid three guineas for the part of Romeo in an amateur production at The Royal Soho Theatre.

It was natural that the professional theatre should

recruit from such sources. Munden first attracted attention in a private performance at the Haymarket theatre, and many famous actors, including Powell, Holland, Parsons, Elliston, Edwin, and Cooke, began in the spouting clubs. So, no doubt, did the less famous Mr. Larken, an engraver by profession, who on May 12, 1772, appeared as Richard for the benefit of Quick. "We hope he *cuts* a better Figure on Copper than he does on the Stage," remarked *The Theatrical Review, or New Companion to the Playhouse.*

It is plain that there was very little barrier in the Georgian theatre between amateur and professional. The enthusiastic spouter found his way on to the professional stage, and, as an insurance against penury, the actor often led a double existence in one of the less romantic professions. Bridgwater (whom Davies esteemed for his playing of Hubert) was a coal-merchant. At Exeter in 1767 one of the managers was "a Thespian butcher . . . who absolutely sold steaks and beef in the morning at his stall and cut up Richard and Macbeth at night on the stage."[14]

In addition to these eccentricities, the Georgian managers, for some reason of patronage, influence or confidence in the attractions of youth, frequently permitted a beginner to attempt a leading part. John Henderson made his debut, and at fashionable, discriminating Bath, in the character of Hamlet; Bensley at Drury Lane in the exacting part of Pierre. A splendid system for the really talented, it was a disastrous one for the Larkens, and a grievous imposition on those who witnessed their performances. "Used as we are to the failure of first appearances," wrote the critic of *The Gazetteer*, January 21, 1780, of a lady who made her debut at Drury Lane in the part of Lady Townly, "we can not help expressing our astonishment that any one person could have been found, who pretended to the least experience or judgment, who had conceived that she possessed any requisites which ought to have encouraged her to attempt acting."

A first appearance seems to have had some special excitement value for the Georgian audience, and the managers gratified their sadistic pleasure even at the expense of strict veracity. "Last night," wrote the *Gazetteer*, February 22, 1780, "a Gentleman, whose name we understand is Bludwick, performed the character of Lear at Covent Garden Theatre, which was announced (according to the usual language on such occasions) as his first appearance on any stage. From the easy and unembarrassed air of his deportment, we much doubt whether it is really his first appearance before an audience, but it is exceedingly clear that it ought to be his last."

These were fatuous practices and at least one man of the theatre denounced them. The elder Sheridan told Boswell on December 13, 1762, that "the taste of the age was terrible. That they would run to see an actor, being his first appearance, eagerly"—and, a hundred and fifty years in advance of his time, he added, "If I was manager of a theatre, nobody should be allowed to come on under seven years of apprenticeship and being regularly taught."[15]

It was certainly not difficult to make a beginning in the Georgian theatre. The story of Nicholas Nickleby tramping to Portsmouth with some vague idea of going to sea, and becoming an actor by accident, can be matched again and again in theatrical biography. Thomas Holcroft had spent his youth as a tramp, a jockey, and a cobbler. Finding himself in London without money, friends, or even a home, he was on his way to enlist as a common soldier in the service of the East India Company, when he met an acquaintance from one of these spouting clubs, who urged him to become an actor instead. Holcroft took his advice, obtained a job in Dublin, and, after seven years' wanderings in the provinces, found his way to London, an inferior engagement at Drury Lane, and eventually to fame as a dramatic author.

Profit prompted the Georgian actor to admit amateurs —but some other excuse must be found for his own amateurish attitude towards rehearsing.

The Georgian theatre mainly depended on a stock of plays. A success went into the repertoire, and since all the plays were familiar to all the actors, very little time was spent in rehearsing them. In every theatre, in the provinces as well as in London, the best parts were recognized as the property of certain actors. In a London theatre even an inferior player delivered his 'cast of characters' to the prompter, who filled in the small parts from his knowledge of the individual claims and capabilities of each actor.

Wherever a star happened to play, he expected to be given his own particular characters. It was a convenient arrangement—not unlike the position which exists today in the world of grand opera—but it was one which led inevitably to jealousies and to a dangerous exaltation of the actor. "Miss Macklin," wrote Thomas Snagg, "had enjoyed some of her characters so many years that it had become disgusting to view her."[16] Elliston, during his early days at the Haymarket, wrote, "Young Bannister, eaten up with spleen, has positively refused my repeating

Sheva, which he claims his unalienable own."[17] Cooke's biographer solemnly remarked that his attempt to play Hamlet while Kemble was out of England was ill-judged. "Hamlet was looked upon as Mr. Kemble's property; and it would be felt, if not thought dishonest, to seize it in his absence."[18] Many years earlier the boot had been on the other leg when Kemble was playing for Tate Wilkinson at York. "I am sure I could not abide to see Mr. Kemble play Hamlet," said Wilkinson's servant, loyally supporting the local star. "You know, sir, it is Mr. Cummins's part."[19] In 1773 there were serious riots at Covent Garden arising from the opposition of Smith's supporters to the playing of Macbeth by Macklin.[20]

When the stars visited resident companies in the provinces, a single rehearsal in the morning was as much as any play in the repertory usually received—just sufficient for the great person to indicate where he wanted people to stand that night to suit his best convenience. That was all the rehearsal that Macready had when he played with Mrs. Siddons in his father's company in 1811. Nor does it appear from Macready's diary that, twenty or even thirty years later, conditions in the provinces had improved in the slightest. When all the credit of a play, and most of the takings, were to be swept up by a visiting star, the local company was not always concerned with perfection. In *Macbeth* at Dublin, in 1832, he notes that the physician "came on too late, half-undressed, holding his clothes." A year or two later at Brighton "in the play of *Sardanapalus* not one person was perfect." At Exeter in 1836, in *Virginius*, one of the Roman decemviri was "so excessively drunk as to tumble from the *sella curulis* into the Forum. . . ." At Exeter again, in 1841, he notes: "Acted Cardinal

Richelieu as well as the wretched murdering of the other characters would let me."

Macready was a notorious growser—but all the memoirs of the Georgian theatre contain the same sort of story. In 1784 Tate Wilkinson's company at York presented *The Devil To Pay* without the leading character. The actor was ill. There was no one to take his place—so the play was put on with the principal part omitted altogether. Kemble and Cooke once played a scene by accident from the third act of *The Gamester* in the middle of Act II—and then put things square by playing the second act scene in Act III; and Fitzball tells an extraordinary tale of the first performance of *Nitocris*, in 1855, when the last two acts of the five act tragedy were not played at all. In 1805 Michael Kelly was several times obliged to drop the curtain at the Opera House in the middle of a ballet, at 12 o'clock on a Saturday night, to meet the orders of the Bishop of London—all due to "never being able to get the lady-singers ready to begin in time."[21]

Sometimes, even in London, a part was read—an imposition which an audience tolerated if they thought the excuse a fair one, and loudly denounced if they thought they were being imposed upon. In 1776 Mrs. Montague, furiously jealous of Mrs. Hudson, refused to study her part in *Henry II* for Mrs. Hudson's benefit at Hull. When the night came, it was announced that Mrs. Montague had been prevented by illness from studying Queen Eleanor and that she begged to read the part. Whereupon the audience informed the lady that if she would not perform the part properly she could depart, "for rather than submit to such intentional insult and effrontery, they would desire the *cook-wench* from the first ale-house to read it—on which she placed herself in an attitude of tragedy, and having obtained a minute's truce—said aloud, 'So I may not be permitted to read the Queen?' 'No, no, no!—off, off, off!'—'Well then,' says she, 'curse you all!' She then threw the book into the pit, and made her exit amidst shouts of disgrace, but not entirely without laughter, from such as smiled at the tumult, and enjoyed the storm. . . ."[22]

That the reading of a part was something often expected in the early eighteenth-century theatre is proved by the statement of Charlotte Charke that it was her "good fortune to be selected from the rest of the Company as Stock-Reader to the Theatre [Drury Lane] in Case of Disasters"—an office in which she acquitted herself "tolerably to the Satisfaction of the Masters and Audience."[23]

There is plenty of other evidence of this feeble practice. Thomas Davies reports that, owing to the failure of a new-comer, a principal character in the Drury Lane production of *Zara* was "forced to be read for several nights together".[24] Munden's biography contains the story of one Hargrave, who was so annoyed at being hissed by a capricious Covent Garden audience that he left the theatre. The house had to put up with the rest of the part being read by someone else. Horace Walpole tops everything in a letter of October 31, 1741, with the startling remark, "Amorevoli is ill and does not sing; his part is to be read." Presumably he meant "sung, book in hand." Two days later he wrote, "They were obliged to omit the part of Amorevoli, who has a fever"—which suggests a performance of remarkable peculiarity.

It is astonishing that the theatre, in the hey-day of its greatest actors, should have been betrayed, and so often betrayed, into such dismal amateurishness. Several letters of Horace Walpole in October and November 1781 describe the rehearsals of *The Count of Narbonne*, an adaptation by Robert Jephson of Walpole's novel *The Castle of Otranto*. At first Harris attempted to produce the play in a fortnight, and it was postponed a week only because Henderson was ill. On November 10 Henderson was still too ill to rehearse, and Lewis did not know two lines of his part. On the 16th Walpole was seeing dresses tried on in the green-room, and directing armour in the painting room, and on the 17th the play was produced—with success, though Lewis was bad and Henderson still far from well.

When Kean first rehearsed Shylock at Drury Lane in 1814, "so little interest seemed to be attached to the event of Mr. Kean's success," writes Thomas Dibdin, "that, through one excuse or other sent by performers for non-attendance, there were, in some scenes, only the new actor, and myself as prompter, on the stage. I apologized to Mr. Kean for this seeming neglect, which he appeared quite indifferent about. . . ."[25]

Actors who regarded rehearsals as superfluous for the plays in the repertoire, were not likely to give a great deal of attention even to a new production. During the production of Sarah Gardner's *The Marriage Advertisement* (1777), all but two of the actors dodged the rehearsals and Edwin, who had not rehearsed at all, was obliged to read his part in performance.[26] Kemble attended only the last three rehearsals of *The Iron Chest* in 1796. Kean refused to appear at any of the last rehearsals of a new play in 1827. Cooke did not get as far as the stage on the first night of a new production in 1803. He was "indisposed".

Even the managers were extraordinarily complacent about rehearsals. "Of course," wrote George Colman to Charles Mathews, "your attendance will be expected in town a week or ten days (as I begin with novelties) previously to the opening of the theatre."[27] A week or ten days was generous. According to Michael Kelly, *The Glorious First of June* (1794) was "all got up in three days,"[28] and Dibdin writes proudly of arrangements at Drury Lane early in the season of 1815—"As the performers seldom meet all together about the commencement of the season, until a day or two before performance, there are very few instances of a novelty's having been produced so early as on a second night; but we had transmitted manuscripts of their respective characters to those who were in the country, convened an early meeting of those who were in town, and left nothing unattended to accomplish the desired object."[29]

This readiness to deal with anything at a moment's notice may sound impressively workmanlike. But things must often have been grotesquely under-rehearsed. The last scene of *The Critic* was unwritten two days before the first performance. The last scene of *Pizarro* was unwritten when the curtain rose on the first night; the parts were distributed during the performance, and allegedly learnt by those famous quick studies.[30] When Fanny Burney's tragedy was produced at Drury Lane in 1795 the performers "were cruelly imperfect. . . . The most important character after the hero and heroine had but two lines of his part by heart! He made all the rest at random, and such nonsense as put all the other actors out as much as himself." Cumberland sent her a significant message via Dr. Burney. He could have told her in advance what would happen from what he had heard behind the scenes. The players had given the play a bad name. They did not intend that it should succeed.[31]

Actors working in the stock theatre were often suspicious of the new work. They had enough to cope with without novelties. At Covent Garden, in 1819, Macready was invited to open with Macduff—follow two days later with Joseph Surface (which he had never played before)—play Rolla on the following Monday, "and to be perfect in the new character of Mordent for the second Wednesday." Macduff he declined—but the other characters were all duly performed. Later in the season he was given one week's warning of the management's intention to present him in the part of Richard III.

These slap-dash methods had grown up understandably from the tradition of the stock company. An actor who had played a part many times before was not likely to play it differently because he had come to London. And the idea of imposing the conceptions of a producer, in the modern sense of the word, had hardly taken root. Rehearsals were conducted partly by the prompter whose book was marked with all the normally accepted business, and partly by the star performer, for even if he were an importation from the provinces, and making his first appearance at a great London theatre, the right of the principal actor to direct his own scenes was unquestioned.

George Frederick Cooke attended rehearsal at Covent Garden for the first time on October 29, 1800. Two days later, on October 31, he made his triumphant appearance as Richard III. The play was not "produced" at all. The actors knew the great plays of the repertoire backwards, and the interest on the night of October 31 was not concerned with any probable novelty of production.

1. Mrs. Siddons, rehearsing with her father and Henderson. *From a water-colour drawing by Thomas Rowlandson.*

2. Actors Rehearsing. *From a water-colour drawing by Thomas Rowlandson.*

The audience came to see the new actor, to judge between George Frederick Cooke and John Philip Kemble.

"None but those who are acquainted with the interior
of a theatre . . . can form an adequate notion of the
anxious feelings experienced on such an occasion."
Cooke's biographer, William Dunlap, is referring to
Cooke's first rehearsal: "The Roscius of the day sees in
the candidate a pretender, who would hurl him from the
throne; and the would-be Roscius a bar, if successful, to
all his great ambition. Every side-wing is thronged with
anxious observers, while the candidate, if a veteran like
Cooke, will perhaps walk through the rehearsal, direct
the business of his scenes, and give no intimation of the
manner he intends to act, or the powers he can display
to the public."[32]

Thomas Dibdin was to make an exactly similar
comment upon Kean's first appearance as Shylock. "He
did not at rehearsal speak so as to convey any very
magnificent idea of what he meant to do."[33] And the
point is again emphasized by Dunlap in a casual reference
to a rehearsal in America, when Cooke and Cooper were
acting together in 1811. "On Friday morning, some
gentlemen by invitation attended rehearsal, which was
conducted with unusual regularity, and some of the
scenes of Othello and Iago played nearly as at night."[34]

In the Georgian theatre there was rivalry between the
two great houses, but it was nothing to the rivalry between the leading actors inside either one of them.
It was hit or miss with that public, and an actor with his
way to make was extremely wary about betraying his
tactics. During the rehearsals of *The Merchant of Venice*
in 1740 Macklin "did not let any person, not even the
players see how he intended to act the part. He merely

C

repeated the lines . . . and did not, by so much as one
single look, tone, gesture, or attitude, disclose his manner
of personating this cruel Israelite"[35]—methods which
could hardly have assisted a general cohesion, but which
undoubtedly redounded to the glory of Macklin, and
provided both cast and audience with the surprise of the
season.

In Garrick's time, Thomas Davies says, "Punctuality
in attendance at rehearsals was exacted and complied
with, and as much due attendance paid to the business
of the scene as during the time of acting a play."[36]
Probably things were at their best when star and manager
were the same person, but even during Garrick's
management plays were inadequately studied. Richard
Cross, the prompter, noted on December 5, 1760, that
the first performance of *Polly Honeycomb* had been in-
differently received, "partly oweing to the Fright and
Confusion of the Performers, who omitted some Speeches
on which the Plot depended".[37]

Munden's biographer says that in his early days (he
came to Covent Garden in 1790) rehearsals were held
frequently and that "it was not unusual to have a dress
rehearsal" when much was expected of a performance.
But, at a later period, a comedy was sometimes read in
the green-room one day, rehearsed the next, and played
the day after. "The performers came upon the scene as
if they had never seen each other before, each intent
upon his particular part only."[38]

Results were sometimes deplorable. "The whole play
went off very flatly—it had been badly rehearsed", wrote
Genest of *The Revenge* at the Bath theatre on December
30, 1816. "Weeks, in the 5th act, spoke a speech P.S. in
expectation that Leonora would enter that way, but she

came on O.P.—of course there was a laugh—Kean had before looked for Carlos the wrong way."

Some years later Genest was commenting on the folly of Miss Dance, a Bath actress, who, through indolence and love of amusement "was frequently in bed when she ought to have been at rehearsal." On April 5, 1823, she dried up in a speech in *The Belle's Stratagem*, which she had refused to rehearse in the morning, saying, "It is a long speech, we will pass it over."

Even at that date things were not much better contrived in London.

"It was the custom of the London actors," writes Macready, "especially the leading ones, to do little more at rehearsals than read or repeat the words of their parts, marking on them their entrances and exits, as settled by the stage manager, and their respective places on the stage. To make any display of passion or energy would be to expose oneself to the ridicule or sneers of the green-room, and few could be more morbidly sensitive to this than myself. But the difficulty of attaining before an audience perfect self-possession, which only practice can give, made me resolve to rehearse with the same earnestness as I would act. . . . Upon making the experiment I may quote Dryden's line, ' 'Tis easy said, but oh! how hardly tried!' I found it much more difficult to force myself to act in the morning with the cold responses and the composed looks of Miss O'Neill, Young, and the rest than at night before the most crowded auditory."[39]

In later life Macready had things as he wanted them—and it is particularly agreeable to find him reporting in his *Recollections* that "Frequently when I have given certain directions to actors rehearsing, the answer has been 'Sir, I never can act at rehearsal, but I will do it at night' "—followed by a serious argument in favour of accurate rehearsing.[40] To this generation "All right on the night" is a famous theatrical joke—a sarcasm aimed at unreliable actors and incompetent production—and here it is, not much more than a century ago, served up as a serious excuse.

Truly the organized theatre is something very nearly new.

REFERENCES

1. *The Private Correspondence of David Garrick*, vol. 2, pp. 42, 121, 106.
2. Thomas Davies, *Memoirs of the Life of David Garrick*, 1780, vol. 1, pp. 339-40.
3. Mrs. Mathews, *Memoirs of Charles Mathews*, 1838, vol. 1, p. 273.
4. Tate Wilkinson, *The Wandering Patentee*, 1795, vol. II, pp. 162, 262.
5. *Diary and Letters of Madame D'Arblay*, 2nd edition, 1842-6, Vol. 2, pp. 184-5. The pagination of the first edition is slightly different, 14 for 17, etc.
6. Sybil Rosenfeld, *Strolling Players and Drama in the Provinces, 1660-1765* (1939), pp. 223, 241, 250, 262, 296-7.
7. *Memoirs of Joseph Sheppard Munden by his Son*, 1844, p. 54.
8. Horace Walpole, *Letters*, Aug. 12, 1790.
9. Wilkinson, *The Wandering Patentee*, vol. 3, p. 15.
10. S. W. Ryley, *The Itinerant*, 1808-27, vol. 3, p. 15. Compare *Memoirs of Charles Lee Lewes*, 1805, vol. 4, p. 179: "Digges, in order to bring a house, had suffered a Mr. Stirling, a fishmonger (a person well known in Edinburgh) to play the part of Iago in *Othello*."
11. *Ibid.*, p. 38.
12. James Boaden, *The Life of Mrs. Jordan*, 1831, vol. 2, p. 120.
13. There is a good description of a spouting club in *The Eccentricities of John Edwin* by Anthony Pasquin, 1791, vol. 1, pp. 5-12. The second act of *The Apprentice* by Arthur Murphy, 1756, is set in a spouting club.
14. Thomas Snagg, *Recollections of Occurrences*, written in 1810, published 1951; p. 55.
15. Boswell, *London Journal*, 1762-3, ed. Frederick A. Pottle, 1950, p. 83. When Mrs. Cibber appeared as Zara, her husband, though it was not her first appearance, delivered a prologue, entreating the clemency of the audience.

> . . . If she conveys the pleasing Passions right,
> Guard and support her this decisive Night.
> If she mistakes, or finds her Strength too small,
> Let interposing Pity break her Fall—
> In you it rests to save her, or destroy.
> If she draws Tears from you—I weep—for joy.

16. Snagg, *op. cit.*, p. 106.

17. George Raymond, *The Life and Enterprises of Robert William Elliston*, 1857 edition, p. 34.

18. William Dunlap, *Memoirs of George Frederick Cooke*, 1813, vol. 1, p. 224.

19. Wilkinson, *The Wandering Patentee*, vol. 2. p. 11.

20. A full report of the suit, which Macklin had the courage to bring against the principals in this discreditable affair, is published in the second volume of James Thomas Kirkman's *Memoirs of the Life of Charles Macklin*, 1799.

21. Michael Kelly, *Reminiscences*, 1826, vol. 2, pp. 230-1.

22. Wilkinson, *The Wandering Patentee*, vol. 1, p. 245. On the practice of reading a part Wilkinson judiciously observes, vol. 3, p. 61: "If the first night of a new play, it must to a certainty destroy the effect for any future representation."

23. *A Narrative of the Life of Mrs. Charlotte Charke*, 1755, reprinted Constable's Miscellany, 1929, p. 53.

24. Davies, *Garrick*, vol. 1, p. 137.

25. Thomas Dibdin, *Reminiscences*, 1827, vol. 2, p. 28.

26. See F. Grice and A. Clarke, "Mrs. Sarah Gardner" in *Theatre Notebook*, vol. 7, No. 4, pp. 76-81, 1953: an article with long verbatim extracts from a newly-discovered eighteenth-century manuscript.

27. Mathews, *op. cit.*, vol. 1, p. 348.

28. Kelly, *op. cit.*, vol. 2, p. 70.

29. Dibdin, *op. cit.*, vol. 2, p. 67.

30. Kelly, *op. cit.*, vol. 2, pp. 162-3, 344.

31. D'Arblay, *op. cit.*, vol. 6, p. 34-5.

32. Dunlap, *op. cit.*, vol. 1, p. 112.

33. Dibdin, *op. cit.*, vol. 2, p. 28.

34. Dunlap, *op. cit.*, vol. 2, p. 290. Compare also Edward Cape Everard, *Memoirs of an Unfortunate Son of Thespis*, 1818, p. 23: "I have heard [Holland] rehearse Zanga in *The Revenge* in the morning, almost in the same loud tones as he would play it at night."

35. Kirkman, *op. cit.*, vol. 1, p. 254.

36. Davies, *Garrick*, vol. 1, p. 111.

37. Dougald MacMillan, *Drury Lane Calendar 1747-1776* (1938), p. 79.

38. Munden, *op. cit.*, p. 307.

39. W. C. Macready, *Reminiscences and Selections from his Diaries and Letters*, ed. Sir Frederick Pollock, 1875, vol. 1, p. 145.

40. *Ibid.*, vol. 1, p. 146.

II

THE LOST ART OF APPLAUSE

"*Mr. Macklin* had no sooner delivered this speech, than the audience burst out into a thunder of applause, and in proportion as he afterwards proceeded to exhibit and mark the malevolence, the villainy, and the diabolical atrocity of the character, so in proportion did the admiring and delighted audience testify their approbation of the Actor's astonishing merit, by still louder plaudits and acclamations, to the end of the Play."

Memoirs of the Life of Charles Macklin
by James Thomas Kirkman, 1799

II

ACTORS of only fifty years ago would be greatly surprised and considerably humiliated by the reception of a twentieth-century audience. Today the public welcomes a favourite artist on his first entry, and applauds an effective exit. But, except for laughter, the general development of a play is followed in a respectful silence. Applause is reserved for the end, and even there it is seldom tumultuous.

Theatrical manners have changed totally. When Quin first played Cato, at the line 'Thanks to the Gods! My boy has done his duty!' the whole house is said to have cried out "Booth outdone! Booth outdone!" In 1763, at Powell's first appearance at Drury Lane, "the audience, not content with clapping, stood up and cheered."[1] Half a century later they were behaving with exactly the same excitable generosity at Macready's first performance of *Richard III* at Covent Garden in 1819. After the words 'Why then my loudest fears are hushed' "the pit rose to a man and continued waving hats and handkerchiefs in a perfect tempest of applause for some minutes."[2]

A twentieth-century actor would be embarrassed by that kind of reception in the course of the play. The old style actor could not do without it—though Joseph Munden, at his first London appearance in 1790, was "for a moment disconcerted" at observing an old Newcastle friend in the pit, standing on a bench, waving his wig above his head, and bawling out "Bravo, Joe Munden!" Mrs. Siddons declared that the punctuation of applause "not only invigorated her whole system, but the space it occasioned, assisted the breath and nerve, which when not relieved by the warmth of the auditors, chills and deadens the mind of the actor." And Henry Irving told American reporters in 1883 that applause was an actor's "life and soul when he is on the stage. The enthusiasm of the audience reacts upon him. He gives them back heat for heat."[3]

Mrs. Siddons practised what she preached. When Macready acted with her as a very new young man in 1811, as she stood by the side-wing, waiting for her cue, she raised her hands and clapped one of his lines loudly, calling out, 'Bravo, sir! Bravo!' This was in sight of the audience and they joined in her applause.

Sometimes—particularly in Dublin—this audience reaction was due more to high spirits than critical enthusiasm. Charles Mathews, in a letter of 1794, describes the custom of the Dublin galleries in calling for applause on a performer's entry—"for instance when *Cherry* enters, the cry is instantly 'A clap for Cherry!' and if anyone displeases them, a groan is called for."[4] Earlier in the century Samuel Foote had noted of the Irish stage that "when the audience was remarkably pleased with any individual passage, they continued applauding (no matter at what state of the play) till the curtain fell, without suffering the whole to be regularly finished."[5]

That sounds strangely, but in London a critical audience often indulged in applause persistent enough to be described as continuous by many observers. Thomas Davies says that Mrs. Abington in *The Chances* kept the audience "in constant good humour and merriment, which they recompensed by the loudest applause, through all the several scenes in which she acted."[6]

At Master Betty's first appearance in London, in 1804, the enthusiasm was so hysterical that as a compliment to the young Roscius, the audience refused to permit the farce to be played. At the farewell performance of Garrick in 1776 and of Mrs. Siddons in 1812 the audience stopped the play as soon as their favourites had completed their parts. In Dublin this compliment was paid to actors who had no thought of retiring. A letter from William Smith to Garrick, June 26, 1774, reports that, at his benefit, he had played "to a very great house, great applause and the repeated compliment of the curtain ordered down at my death". On another night, when *Jane Shore* was played, the curtain was ordered down in honour of Mrs. Hartley.[7] At Bath on July 12, 1816, when Kean was carried off in the last scene of *A New Way to Pay Old Debts* "a Gentleman in the Pit called out for the Curtain to fall", writes Genest; "the absurd motion was seconded by others, and the piece was brought to an abrupt conclusion—this was the more improper, as on the 2nd of July Stanley had spoken the last speech particularly well."

In 1814 Hazlitt reported that, at Kean's first appearance in London as Shylock, "the applause, from the first scene to the last, was general, loud, and uninterrupted"; and that "almost every passage was received with equal and deserved applause."[8] It was just the same twenty years later. According to Edward Fitzball, Mrs. West in *Esmeralda* (1834) was received with "a continuous burst of applause from the beginning of her scenes to their termination." And when Nicholas Nickleby acted at Miss Snevellicci's great bespeak (on a date unspecified, but reported by Charles Dickens in 1838) he was accorded a round of applause every time he spoke, which rose to a tumult at that splendid moment when Mrs. Crummles (who was his unworthy mother) sneered and called him 'presumptious boy'.

Sometimes applause was given for the speaking of a single line. John O'Keefe remarks that old Sheridan's manner of saying 'I could be merry now, Hubert', "got him most abundant applause".[9] And Leigh Hunt, in an adverse criticism, observes that "everybody applauds Mrs. Powell in her delivery" of the exclamation 'Was he alive?' in *Douglas*, "but everybody knows that she copies it exactly from Mrs. Siddons."[10]

Applause was often provoked by some effective piece of business. Hazlitt says that in *Richard III* Kean's "manner of bidding his friends goodnight, and his pausing with the point of his sword, drawn slowly backward and forward on the ground . . . received shouts of applause." And the action of pointing his finger at himself when complaining that he was 'scarce half made-up' produced a round of applause which broke into his speech.[8]

A round of applause, in the singular, is a phrase still accepted in the playhouse. In the Georgian theatre there seem to have been rounds, in the plural, the number nicely calculated to reflect degrees of enthusiasm. For instance, Charles Rice records that there were "three distinct rounds of applause" on November 25, 1836, after Macready had spoken the line

> Wake Duncan with thy knocking! I would thou coulds't!

"Distinct" can only suggest that it had been possible to detect three successive waves of sound. Again, on December 17, 1836, Charles Kemble's 'Queen Mab' speech received "three rounds of well-merited applause", while a feat in *Hassan Pasha* on March 11, 1837 "was honoured with four tremendous rounds".[11] Charles Mathews and George Frederick Cooke were each accorded as many as six.[12]

These orgies of enthusiasm must have had a most peculiar effect both upon the sense, and the artistic shape, of a play. At a performance of *Richard III*, May 2, 1837, Rice noted that "the touchstone of the character

'Off with his head',

was marred by a too speedy round of applause, for the approbation began at the conclusion of the words I have quoted, and the point which must follow in

'So much for Buckingham',

was inaudible." A month later, at a performance of *Othello*, June 6, 1837, an absurd vacuum was caused by the *absence* of applause. "Mr. E. F. Saville," wrote Rice, "is a moderately good representative of Cassio, but he should rather let his first speech on entering be stopped by applause than stand and look foolish in expecting it; an audience do not always recognize a new performer on the instant."[13]

It is certain that actors not only expected applause but expected it at regular and recognized places. Right at the end of his career Macready made an angry note in his diary, of a performance of *Hamlet*, that "the audience gave less applause to the first soliloquy than I am in the habit of receiving."[14] A man accustomed to applause throughout the whole course of a play was naturally extremely put out if he did not get it, and without doubt occasions were carefully designed for exciting it. Actors played for it. Authors wrote for it. Fitzball, in his memoirs, tells an illuminating story about his engagement

by Elliston to liven up *The Somnambulist*. "At length,"
he writes, "at the scene where the Count goes out at the
window, and where I had contrived to pop into his
mouth a clap-trap, respecting what the man deserves
who would be coward enough to take advantage of
unprotected female innocence, Elliston smiled one of his
George-the-Fourth smiles, and exclaimed, rubbing his
hands, exultingly—'That will do, sir, that will do; now
we *shall* bring them down!' "[15]

Clap-trap: nowadays that word is used to describe
any windy rhetorical nonsense. A hundred years ago
Fitzball was using the word in its original theatrical
sense. Two hundred years ago, Aaron Hill was using it
seriously, explaining gravely in a letter to Mallet, dated
December 21, 1741, how a writer of skill should prepare
"in all his *strong*, or his *passionate* speeches, as many
Clap-traps, for the most part, as *couplets*." He then prints
nine and a half lines of verse and inserts five asterisks in
them. If the actor, says he, would only pause at these
points "as many *claps* would infallibly follow, and throw
the *house* into an *uproar of pleasure*."

In 1746 this solemn prig addressed himself to Garrick,
sending him the first act of a tragedy, with the assurance
that it contained more than thirty places where the actor
would receive general applause "to popular and generous
sentiments." A year or two later he is still on the same
subject—kindly offering to show more than seventy
places in the part of Cato, where—if Garrick will be
ruled by him—"*strong claps* would rise, infallibly."[16]

The fate of a play in the twentieth century is decided
by the public bookings made over several days following
the first night. In the eighteenth and early nineteenth
centuries the verdict was given at the time, in the

theatre, and by the audience. At the end of the play an actor was appointed to come before the curtain and, as the phrase went, "give out the play for repetition." "Ladies and Gentlemen, under the sanction of your kind approbation," he would begin—and then, as Thomas Dibdin remarks, "The Ayes and Noes generally interrupt the remainder."[17] Whether the play was abandoned or continued largely depended on the caprice of that first audience.

This ancient practice of speaking before the curtain at the end of the play is the origin of the actor's curtain call. Kean was the first actor to receive the compliment—after the first performance of *Brutus; or the Fall of Tarquin* on December 3, 1818; but it was Macready, ten months later, who recorded the new procedure in his diary.

After his performance of Richard III at Covent Garden on October 25, 1819, "the pit rose with one accord, waving their hats with long-continued cheers; nor with the fall of the curtain did the display of enthusiasm relax. Connor, who played Tyrrel, the actor appointed, was not allowed to give out the play, and the practice was this evening first introduced of calling on the principal actor. [First introduced at Covent Garden, he means.] In obedience to the impatient and persevering summons of the house, I was desired by Fawcett to go before the curtain; and accordingly I announced the tragedy for repetition." The same thing happened a month later, after his performance as Coriolanus. "Mr. Egerton," wrote the reporter of *The Morning Herald*, "came on to announce the next performance, but was obliged to give way for a general cry of Macready."[18]

The groundlings enjoyed this familiarity with the star actor. The critics did not. "He was even called for," complained *The Times* after *Richard III*, "according to the practice adopted at, and hitherto we had hoped confined to, the other theatre. . . ."

It was to be a long time before the critics accepted the curtain call. After Kean's performance of Coriolanus in 1820, *The Times* (January 26) was still mumbling about "the absurdity of the reanimation of Mr. Kean to announce the repetition of the tragedy tomorrow"; and sixteen years later Charles Rice was making exactly similar comments in his "Dramatic Register". Rice was no literary critic, but he had the invaluable habit of recording what he saw. Should an actor be hissed, or prompted, should the scenery be bungled, or the house talkative, should the overture be encored or the performance over-long, Rice would be sure to note it all down, as though he knew that these gossipy details would be more valuable to future students of the theatre than any attempt he could make at real dramatic criticism.

From Rice's reviews alone it can be plainly proved that the curtain call was still not accepted routine in 1836–7 and that it was frequently resented by the judicious. Again and again Rice takes the trouble to mention the names of the performers called, and there are never more than three in a cast. Sometimes he notes that the call was not taken up by the house—"There was a trifling call for Phillips, but the audience had too much sense to second it, and the matter dropped." (January 28, 1837.) Sometimes the call was not answered—"The fall of the curtain was attended by thunders of applause, and a call for Mr. Macready; but he declined the 'honour' of appearing any more that evening." (November 25, 1836.) Sometimes the compliment was omitted because the leading actor was not liked, and sometimes there was no

3. Rachel, on the stage of Her Majesty's Theatre, on the last night of the season, 1841. *From a water-colour by Eugène Louis Lami.*

call because no one had thought of starting it. Thus, in spite of Vandenhoff's success as William Tell, "the ridiculous practice of calling a principal performer before the curtain at the conclusion of the play was on this occasion abandoned." (April 8, 1837.) It was evidently an unusual omission, for only a few months later Rice remarks of Phelps's call after a performance of *Hamlet*, that the practice "is now so common, that its award is complied with more from fear of damping an actor's spirits by non-observance of so ridiculous a custom, than as a reward of out-of-the-way histrionic display." (August 28, 1837.)[19]

That sentence sounds conclusive; but it is significant that *The Times*, five years later (October 25, 1842), was careful to record that "the principal actors were called for" after Macready's successful *King John*. By then twenty-four years had passed since Kean's original call on December 3, 1818, but the appearance of the actors before the curtain was still 'news'; and seventeen years later William B. Wood (who had seen Kean take the first recorded curtain call at Philadelphia in 1821) was still protesting against "the habit of calling out performers, *dead or alive*, after the curtain has dropped, to receive a tribute of extra applause. . . . It has always been a matter of wonder with me that the better part of the audience should tolerate such fooleries. Can anything be more ridiculous, than that an actor, after labouring through an arduous character—a combat, and the whole series of simulated expiring agonies, should instantly revive, and appear panting before the curtain to look and feel like a fool, and to destroy the little illusion which he has been endeavouring to create?"[20]

It is clear that during the reigns of Kean and Macready

D

the curtain call, and the normal announcement at the end of the play, were sometimes the same thing. It is important, therefore, that the two things should not be confused.

For instance, the manager had long been accustomed to come before the curtain on the last night of the season "to return thanks". There was no curtain call about that: it was merely precautionary flattery of the audience. Sometimes a call was made which was not complimentary. "Kemble was called on at the close," writes Boaden of an opera which failed at Drury Lane in the season 1800–1; but it was not as an actor that he came, and not to receive applause. He came as a manager and to announce that the piece would be withdrawn. Again, writing of Mrs. Jordan's benefit at Drury Lane in 1788, Boaden notes in his *Life of Kemble*: "There was one gracefully pleasing event when the curtain fell; Mrs. Jordan came herself forward, and with the most respectful interest gave out the benefit of Mrs. Siddons. She then withdrew to dress for her original part of Matilda in the lovely entertainment of *Richard Coeur de Lion*."[21] Here is a star performer coming before the curtain thirty years before Kean. But Mrs. Jordan came forward as a friendly gesture to Mrs. Siddons. It was her own idea, not the audience's, and her action was plainly unexpected.

Perhaps the last sentence of Boaden's short comment contains a valuable clue to this problem. Mrs. Jordan withdrew to dress for yet another part. Calls, bows, acknowledgements are final things; but in the old theatre, the play of the evening was not the end. Sometimes dances followed, sometimes songs. There was always a farce. Macklin was in the habit of playing Shylock and Sir Archy McSarcasm on the same night.

George Frederick Cooke played Sir Archy with Shylock, Lear, Lord Townly, Oakly, Joseph Surface, Iago, Glenalvon, and Alexander. Elliston, Cherry, and Munden all acted in the play and in the farce on their first appearances in London; and Miss Reeve, on the occasion of "her first appearance on any stage", not only appeared as Ophelia but afterwards as Mary in *The Turnpike Gate*. There was plenty to do in the Georgian theatre, and with the actors busy changing for the next play, and the audience looking forward to the next part of their entertainment, it would not have been natural to indulge in an enthusiasm which too greatly interrupted the sequence of events.

The practice of calling for the author came later. In 1601 when Dekker attacked Ben Jonson in *Satiromastix*, Jonson (in the character of Horace) is forced to make several promises about his future behaviour. One of the charges runs as follows: "Besides, you must forsweare to venter on the stage, when your play is ended, and to exchange curtezies and complements with gallants in the lordes roomes, to make all the house rise up in armes, and to cry that's Horace, that's he, that's he, that pennes and purges humours and diseases." Evidently Ben Jonson liked to be seen, and an Elizabethan stage was easy of access. But showing off is not the same thing as being called upon the stage by the audience. Horace Walpole professed surprise at Richard Bentley even showing his face at the first performance of *The Wishes* in 1761. "All the impudence of false patriotism never came up to it! Did one ever hear of an author that had courage to see his own first night in public? I don't believe Fielding or Foote himself ever did—and this was the modest, bashful Mr. Bentley, that died at the thought of being known for an author even by his own acquaintance."[22]

Horace Walpole might have known that Addison, Steele, and Johnson had been at the first performances of their plays, but in spite of inaccuracy there was something of truth in his sweeping astonishment. There was still a tendency among authors to conceal themselves on a first night. Goldsmith was unable to witness *She Stoops to Conquer*, and General Burgoyne seems not to have been at the first night of *The Maid of the Oaks* on November 5, 1774. He was there on November 8, and found "a general relish was very discernible" in the audience. But his letter to Garrick of November 9 makes no reference to the first performance and states plainly that he does not wish to be recognized as author even among the cast.[23]

Six years later Lady Craven's comedy, *The Miniature Picture*, was played at Drury Lane. She was present on the second night, and Horace Walpole was again surprised even at that. "The chief singularity," he wrote to Mason, May 28, 1780, "was that she went to it herself the second night, in form; sat in the middle of the front row of the stage-box, much dressed, with a profusion of white bugles and plumes to receive the public homage due to her sex and loveliness." He does not say due to her authorship. Later in the letter he remarks that, though civil, the audience had missed an opportunity of being gallant. When her ladyship's name was mentioned, either in the prologue or the epilogue, he forgets which, "they did not applaud as they ought to have done exceedingly when she condescended to avow her pretty child, and was there looking so very pretty."

Apparently Walpole did not consider an epilogue an equally serious embarrassment. He did not flinch from being present on February 17, 1775, at the first performance of his epilogue to Robert Jephson's *Braganza*.

On the night of August 9, 1777, after the first (and last) performance of *The Marriage Advertisement* at the Haymarket, the author, Sarah Gardner, addressed the audience. "She then made her *curtsy*, and her exit was crown'd with every mark of approbation. . . ."[24] This sounds like an author's curtain call, but it was not. Mrs. Gardner was only on the stage because she happened to be one of the cast. No one had called for her. It was she who came forward of her own determination, in pursuit of a quarrel she was engaged upon with the manager and the rest of the company. The audience were giving their support to an injured woman, not to a successful playwright.

It was nearly sixty years later that Charles Dickens made his memorable bow at the St. James's Theatre after the fall of the curtain on *The Village Coquettes* on December 6, 1836.[25] The opera had not been particularly successful —but all the principals paraded before the curtain, followed by John Hullah, the composer. And then, the audience, determined to get a sight of the remarkable young man who had created *Pickwick*, began to scream for Boz; and "to our utter amazement," wrote the critic of *The Morning Herald*, "after some five minutes' uproar, the green curtain again waved, was drawn back—the Boz became manifest." The critics were profoundly shocked. "*The Pickwick Papers* have made him . . . an especial favourite with us; and we have no idea of his being exhibited gratis," wrote John Forster. And the critic of *The Literary Gazette* desired to know when "this ridiculous nonsense" would end.[26]

It was the unprecedented appearance of the author

on the stage that disgusted them. Dickens was not the first
author to acknowledge applause: but the others had done
so from the House, from their seat in a box, as an act of
politeness, not as a piece of exhibitionism. "Will they
have Bulwer on the stage at Covent Garden next Wednesday at the close of *La Vallière*?" demanded *The Literary
Gazette*. "Why did they not Serjeant Talfourd after *Ion*?"

The answer to that question is on record in Macready's
diary. It was only Talfourd's modesty, it seems, and
Macready's obvious jealousy, which prevented the author
of *Ion* from forestalling Dickens by six months.

After describing his own reception before the curtain,
Macready writes, "Miss Ellen Tree, I heard, was afterwards called forward. Talfourd came into my room and
heartily shook hands with me, and thanked me. He said
something about Mr. Wallack wishing him to go on the
stage, as they were calling, but it would not be right.
I said 'On no account in the world'. He shortly left me,
and as I heard, was made to go forward to the front of
his box, and receive the enthusiastic tribute of the house's
grateful delight."[27]

It was a long time before this calling the author was
established as normal practice. Writing of his *Walter
Tyrrel*, produced in 1837, Fitzball remarked on "the
performers being all called before the curtain." But in
those days, he adds, "it was not the fashion to call for
the author; and indeed, I think it much better 'in the
breach than the observance'; authors, like violets, are
best under the leaves." When Sheridan Knowles's play
Love was greeted with cries of 'Author!' in 1839, the
critic of *The Age* denounced "a vulgar custom"—and
Fitzball, who was shy and detested making a bow, was
still using the same adjective twenty years later, when he

wrote in his autobiography of "the vulgar feeling of calling for the author to have a *stare* at him."[28]

In our own time the business of calling for the players —sometimes before the curtain, more often on a full stage—has become an exacted tribute, a thing even rehearsed, a thing organized by the stage rather than demanded by the audience. However bad the play, the curtain flies up on a bowing and smiling cast. The author's call has remained a little more honest. Some authors dislike appearing; and no author would wish to go forward to an uncertain welcome. In 1904 Gilbert refused to bow at the first night of *The Fairy's Dilemma*. "The better class of dramatic authors have agreed not to do so," he noted.[29] Apparently many had been lured on by plaudits and boo-ed off by humorists in the gallery. Henry James met such treatment. So, in recent memory, have others.

The regulated curtain calls of the modern theatre are all of them gigantic clap-traps. A hundred years ago no actors would have dared to take the approbation of the public so much for granted. There was greater sincerity and more fun in that old theatre, where an actor had to fight for success at every performance. Even Mrs. Siddons at the height of her fame played to rowdy houses and sometimes to unappreciative ones. "Farewell, ye brutes!" she said when the curtain fell at Leeds. "And for ever I trust: ye shall never torture me again, be assured."[30] When an audience could so distress a great artist, its approbation must have been doubly sweet. It is true that there were claques—but the amount of genuine enthusiasm was infinitely greater than it is today. Certainly it must have been gratifying to an author to be called to bow "after some five minutes uproar" and far more agreeable than the modern habit of keeping the poor man shivering in the wings to be poked on at the smallest sound of approbation.

A hundred years ago a theatre was alive on both sides of the footlights, and in many ways the audience was as well organized as the stage. The modern audience is passive. It is composed of spectators who watch the play as individuals, not as men linked by a common excitement. The fact that the ladies in the pit and the gallery used to be cast into a frenzy by the mere sight of Lewis Waller (1860–1915) is not to the point. That was never the applause of an audience critically appreciating skilful acting. It was a cult, it was worship.

The modern audience comes to be amused—not to criticize. It cannot compare one man's Macbeth with another's, for it may be years before the opportunity arises of seeing a different production. Under the direction of that newest officer of the theatre, the producer, the modern stage is drilled like an army: but the modern audience has no corporate organization. It is reported both of Kean and of Macready that they were sometimes called before the play began—and at least once each came before the curtain after changing his clothes and taking his paint off. The audience had waited all the time, calling and calling. No twentieth-century theatre-goer is going to sit clapping for ten minutes in order to induce its favourites to step forward. If the actors want to take a call they must look sharp about it. Other things besides their glory have already taken hold of the audience's mind—such as buses and taxis, and the last train home.

REFERENCES

1. Walpole, Oct. 17, 1763.
2. Macready, *op. cit.*, vol. 1, p. 196.
3. Laurence Irving, *Henry Irving*, 1950, p. 421.
4. Mathews, *op. cit.*, vol. 1, p. 96.
5. William Cooke, *Memoirs of Samuel Foote*, 1805, vol. 1, p. 86.
6. Davies, *Garrick*, vol. 1, p. 188.
7. *The Private Correspondence of David Garrick*, 1831-2, vol. 1, p. 639.
8. William Hazlitt, *A View of the English Stage*, collected works, 1903, vol. 8, pp. 179-83.
9. John O'Keefe, *Recollections*, 1826, p. 359.
10. Leigh Hunt, *Critical Essays on the Performers of the London Theatres*, p. 47.
11. Charles Rice, *The London Theatre in the Eighteen-Thirties*, ed. Arthur Colby Sprague and Bertram Shuttleworth for the Society for Theatre Research, 1950, pp. 74, 78, 80.
12. Mathews, *op. cit.*, vol. 1, p. 129; and Dunlap, *op. cit.*, vol. 2, p. 41.
13. Rice, *op. cit.*, pp. 44, 57.
14. Macready, *op. cit.*, vol. 2, p. 270.
15. Edward Fitzball, *Thirty-five Years of a Dramatic Author's Life*, 1859, vol. 1, p. 120.
16. *The Works of the Late Aaron Hill*, 2nd edition, 1754, vol. 2, pp. 184, 264, 360. See also p. 165, below.
17. Dibdin, *op. cit.*, vol. 1, p. 7. Cf. Horace Walpole, July 28, 1761, "It was given out for tonight with more claps than hisses".
18. Macready, *op. cit.*, vol. 1, pp. 196-8.
19. Rice, *op. cit.*, pp. 17, 74, 37, 70. Cf. also: "Mr. Forrest was called for, and went through the usual ridiculous formalities—appearing, bending, and retiring—amidst the most vehement cheering." (p. 6); "Mr. Forrest was not called before the curtain." (p. 27); "He [Phelps] was loudly applauded in many parts of his performance, and called before the curtain at the end of the fourth act." (p. 67.)
20. William B. Wood, *Personal Recollections of the Stage*, 1855, p. 261.
21. James Boaden, *The Life of Mrs. Jordan*, vol. 2, p. 63; and *The Life of John Philip Kemble*, 1825, vol. 1, p. 395.
22. Walpole, July 28, 1761.
23. *The Private Correspondence of David Garrick*, vol. 2, pp. 17-18.
24. See F. Grice and A. Clarke, *Theatre Notebook*, vol. 7, No. 4, p. 80.
25. French authors had taken calls much earlier. Dr. W. J. Lawrence has pointed out a single instance in London of a choreographer taking a call. This was as early as 1788 when Noverre was brought on at the Opera-House after the ballet *Cupid and Psyche*. See *Old Theatre Days and Ways*, 1935, p. 31.
26. The critical comments upon this remarkable occasion may be read together in *The Dickensian*, Summer, 1936, in an article by Walter Dexter.
27. Macready, *op. cit.*, vol. 2, p. 32.
28. Fitzball, *op. cit.*, vol. 1, p. 17; vol. 2, p. 103.
29. Sidney Darke and Rowland Grey, *W. S. Gilbert, His Life and Letters*, 1923, p. 143.
30. Mathews, *op. cit.*, vol. 1, p. 274.

III

NOT A DRY EYE IN THE HOUSE

"I would go to the play twice a week if I could: I dote upon it. Only you're too affecting sometimes. You do put me in such a state; into such fits of crying."

Mrs. Borum to Miss Snevellicci:
Nicholas Nickleby

III

THE ENGLISH are generally supposed to be an unemotional people.* We do not easily weep or cry out. Except in football crowds, outside Buckingham Palace, or in the presence of American film stars, we are reserved and disciplined. We used not to be so. When Sir Robert Walpole took his leave of George II, in 1742, the King fell upon his neck and wept and kissed him.[1] The Duke of Newcastle, on another occasion, prostrated himself full length before the royal feet, sobbing and crying to such an extent that Lord Coventry begged the standers-by to retire with "For God's sake, gentlemen, don't look at a great man in distress."[2] And at George II's funeral, he "fell into a fit of crying the moment he came into the chapel, and flung himself back in a stall, the Archbishop hovering over him with a smelling-bottle— but in two minutes his curiosity got the better of his hypocrisy, and he ran about the chapel with his glass to spy who was or was not there, spying with one hand, and mopping his eyes with t'other."[3]

The Duke of Newcastle was a figure of fun. But stronger men were not better controlled. "Here have been Lord Hartington, Coke, and poor Fitzwilliam, and others crying," wrote Horace Walpole on the occasion of Sir Robert's fall from office.[4] And nearly fifty years later he recorded of a debate in the House of Commons:

* I did not come across the essay on Tears in T. H. White's *The Age of Scandal* (1950) until long after this chapter had been completed. The two essays confirm rather than repeat each other. Only twice do they make use of the same quotations.

"Prodigious clamours and interruptions arose from Mr. Fox's friends, but he, though still applauding the French, burst into tears and lamentations on the loss of Burke's friendship and endeavoured to make atonement; but in vain, though Burke wept too."[5]

In the twentieth century, which contains so much to make men weep, tears have become a private indulgence. Today we are all so hardened that we do not easily believe that men and women ever wept in the way that early novelists have suggested. But the briefest examination of the facts discloses that they certainly did. The friends and family of Fanny Burney, for instance, were in a frequent state of emotional purgation. Dr. Burney confessed that he blubbered at a scene in *Evelina* (1778) and "Lady Hales and Miss Crossmaker are not yet recovered from hearing it; it made them quite ill." Then when *Cecilia* followed in 1782, Charlotte Burney was unable to eat her dinner and had a violent headache all day; Miss Benson was "blind with crying"; Lord de Ferrars "cried violently"; and Mrs. Chapone was heard to say, "Cry, to be sure, we did. O Mrs. Delany, shall you ever forget how we cried?"[6]

Richardson's *Clarissa* seems to have worked a like dissolution upon Aaron Hill in 1748. "I buried the dear girl by three o'clock this morning," he writes to the author, "and I now can hardly see the pen wherewith I tell you that you put my eyes out—and you do it, in so many places, and by such successive, unaccountably astonishing, and not to be resisted strokes of nature, that I really think, in this one single night your heavenly sweet *Clarissa*, and her fate, have cost me tears enough to swim the volumes that excited them."[7]

Almost a hundred years later a tough customer like

Macready could write in the same vein about *The Old Curiosity Shop*. "I saw one print in it of the dear dead child that gave a dead chill through my blood. I dread to read it, but I must get it over." Later in the same day, having braced himself to the ordeal, he wrote in his diary, "I have never read printed words that gave me so much pain. I could not weep for some time. Sensation, sufferings, have returned to me, that are terrible to awaken; it is real to me; I cannot criticize it."[8]

It is not so much the tears as the pleased reporting of them which is foreign to the temperament of the twentieth century. Dr. Burney wept on receiving a letter from Hannah More, saying she had been ill. Tears swam in Dr. Johnson's eyes as he read Dr. Beattie's *Hermit*. Boswell "several times burst into tears" on hearing in the Hebrides the particulars of the '45 rebellion; and Fanny Burney, when Madame D'Arblay, declared that she found a pleading on behalf of the French emigrés so affecting that she was "almost ill from restraining my nearly convulsive emotions."

Tears in the eighteenth century were nothing to be ashamed of. That they should have flowed with particular generosity in the theatre was to be expected.

Aaron Hill, a flabby poet and an unsuccessful playwright, knew all about the emotions. In 1731 he wrote to Mallet after reading *Eurydice* to his family circle; "I wish you had been a witness to the tears it occasioned in a little *audience*, which my family composed about me. They would have warranted at once the sincerity of my opinion, and the future success of your tragedy in its representation; when if you mark a dry eye during many of your moving scenes, you may conclude it the sign of great ignorance of humanity."[9]

'Not a dry eye in the house.' How interesting
it is, and pleasant, to find the germ of that famous
theatrical cliché in a serious criticism more than two
hundred years ago.

In a letter to an actress in 1733 Hill describes how
the mere articulation of the name 'Aboan' "would have
afforded Mrs. *Porter* an occasion of forcing tears from the
most *knowing* part of the audience, and a thunder of
applause from the most numerous."[10] To which may be
added the comment of Garrick's biographer, Thomas
Davies: "When, on leaving Castalio, in the last act
[Mrs. Barry] burst out into that affecting exclamation
'O poor Castalio!' she never failed to shed tears herself,
nor was it possible for the Audience to refrain from
correspondent lamentations."[11]

In another letter of 1733 Hill makes a casual reference
to "several gentlemen in the boxes [who] *laugh'd aloud* at
another gentleman's *tears*."[12] It is likely that tears may
not have been fashionable among the chatterers and
exhibitionists. But they came easily and naturally to the
audience which had come to hear the play. "I could not
help weeping with the heroine of the stage," Roderick
Random confessed; "though I practised a great many
shifts to conceal this piece of impolite *weakness*."

According to Charlotte Charke, Miss Ibbott as Isabella
in *The Fatal Marriage* "not only drew the Audience into
a most profound Attention, but absolutely into a general
Flood of commiserating Tears; and blended Nature and
Art so exquisitely well, that 'twas impossible not to feel
her Sorrows, and bear the tenderest Part in her Afflic-
tion." Mrs. Charke was prompting, and was so affected
herself that she was "rendered incapable of reading a
single Syllable; but luckily, for Miss Ibbott, she is always

London. Printed for Bowles & Carver. No. 69 St. Pauls Church Yard.

AT A TRAGEDY.

125 Dighton del.

5. *From a water-colour by Robert Dighton.*

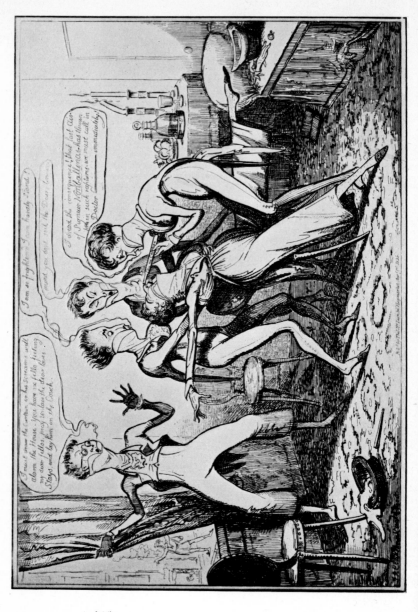

6. A Dandy Fainting. From an etching by Isaac Robert Cruikshank.

so perfect, a Prompter is a useless Person while she is speaking."[13]

In the Garrick biography Davies makes a curious little defence of an Englishman's tears. The French he declares, "are taught to cry habitually at scenes of distress. The Englishman looks upon the theatre as a place of amusement; he does not expect to be alarmed with terror, or wrought upon by scenes of commiseration, but he is surprised into the feelings of these passions and sheds tears because he cannot avoid it."[14] And so men wept at Garrick in *King Lear*: they wept at Barry and Mrs. Cibber in *The Orphan*: they even wept when Mrs. Pritchard played Lady Capulet in order to introduce Miss Pritchard as Juliet. "The daughter's timidity," writes Davies, "was contrasted by the mother's apprehensions, which were strongly painted in their looks, and these were incessantly interchanged by stolen glances at each other. This scene of mutual sensibility was so affecting, that many of the audience burst into involuntary tears."[15]

The records of the eighteenth century are full of such comments. Benjamin Victor describes the apology which the elder Sheridan was forced to make from the Dublin stage in 1755. He was never in the wrong, but he made his submission so well, that "tears gushed from the Eyes of several of his male Auditors."[16]

Fanny Burney in 1780 recorded of the Bath theatre that "two young ladies, who seemed about eighteen, and sat above us, were so much shocked by the death of Douglas, that they both burst into a loud fit of roaring, like little children, and sobbed on, afterwards, for almost half the farce."[17]

It was at the Bath theatre that Frederick Reynolds's first play, *Werther*, was produced in 1785. Many tears had

E

been shed at a private reading of the play in London. "Lady Effingham totally unable to speak . . . as if more astonished than afflicted; Eliza, more afflicted than astonished, with her eyes still drowned in tears, vainly endeavoured to smother in her handkerchief her sighs and sobs."

Equally gratifying results were provoked in the citizens of Bath. "In the first act," says Reynolds, "we knew that the handkerchiefs were in full request. . . . In the garden scene, where Albert and Charlotte mutually endeavour to compose *Werther*, we were delighted by the sound of the first fit, and by the scent of its usual concomitant, hartshorn. Shortly afterwards, I saw, from the stagedoor, one of the principal female competitors in singularity and affectation, conveyed, in a highly interesting state of graceful insensibility, from one of the side boxes. . . . In the scene of the readings from Ossian . . . three more fainted."[18]

To the critical Miss Burney and the sharp-eyed Mr. Reynolds such scenes may have appeared as amusing provincial curiosities: but it was not different in London: "No play ever produced more tears," wrote Horace Walpole, November 18, 1781, to Robert Jephson, author of *The Count of Narbonne*; and "We seldom ever witnessed more tears in a theatre," wrote a critic in 1791, reporting on the first performance of George Colman's *The Surrender of Calais*. "A *young* lady in the Pit was carried out in hysterics: and the *English Character* was well shewn in stopping the performance while humanity was doing its office to a female."[19]

An eighteenth-century audience thought nothing of stopping the show—and 'stopping the show' did not indicate that minute of triumphant success which it means today. The audience stopped the show because it disliked the play, because it had been offended by an actor, or because it did not like the price of admission: and it believed unreservedly in its inalienable right to behave as badly as it wished. When it rioted against the French players at the Haymarket in 1738, ignoring the King's command and obstructing the magistrate, it was solemnly claimed that "the Audience had a legal Right to show their Dislike of any Play or Actor," and "that the Judicature of the Pit had been acknowledged and acquiesced to, Time immemorial."[20]

Sometimes the audience intervened for wholly un-expected reasons of propriety. After the second day of Kean's Richard III, Hazlitt writes that the announcement of the repetition of this tremendous performance was greeted with cries of "No, No" from every point of the house—testifying "the sense entertained by the audience of the impropriety of requiring the repetition of this extraordinary effort till every physical disadvantage had been completely removed."[21] On another occasion the audience intervened during the performance of *Tamerlane* to protect Mrs. Siddons from what they regarded as an outrageous demand upon the delicate nervous system of a lady. Macready tells the story in his *Reminiscences*. "In the last act, when, by order of the tyrant, her lover Monesis is strangled before her face, she worked herself up to such a pitch of agony, and gave such terrible reality to the few convulsive words she tried to utter, as she sank a lifeless heap before her murderer, that the audience for a few moments remained in a hush of astonishment as if awe-struck; they then clamoured for the curtain to be dropped, and insisting on the manager's appearance, received from him, in answer to their vehement inquiries,

the assurance that Mrs. Siddons was alive, and recovering
from the temporary indisposition that her exertions had
caused. They were satisfied as regarded her, but would
not suffer the performance to be resumed."[22]

An equally significant story is told by Macready of the
first, and last, performance of *Fredolfo* by Maturin in
1819. In this play the hero is tricked into giving up his
sword, and is then stabbed with it—a piece of treachery
which so outraged the pit that it "got up with a perfect
yell of indignation, such as, I fancy, was never before
heard in a theatre. . . . The curtain fell in a tumult of
opposition. *Fredolfo* was never acted again."[23]

The twentieth-century audience has grown polite. It
never interrupts the players, and it hardly ever boos.
But how much has it lost in sensitivity? The audience of
Garrick and Mrs. Siddons were not merely witnesses of
a performance: they were a part of it, sharing the joys
and griefs of hero and heroine. When Mrs. Siddons
appeared at Drury Lane in 1782, says the *Biographica
Dramatica*, "The excellence of her performance was
acknowledged and applauded by every person in the
house; but the surest test of its merit was the universal
sympathy of the spectators in the distresses of the heroine,
evinced, not only by copious streams of tears, but
several ladies were actually thrown into fits by the
'cunning of the scene.' "[24]

In that same season of 1782–3 Mrs. Siddons performed
Jane Shore, and "I well remember," wrote James
Boaden, "(how is it possible I should ever forget?) the
sobs, the *shrieks*, among the tenderer part of her audiences;
or those tears, which manhood, at first, struggled to
suppress, but at length grew proud of indulging. We then
indeed knew all the LUXURY of grief; but the nerves of

many a gentle being gave way before the intensity of such appeals: and fainting fits, long and frequently alarmed the decorum of the house, filled almost to suffocation."[25]

There is no discounting the innumerable reports of Mrs. Siddons' command of fits and weeping. Horace Walpole, who remembered Mrs. Porter, could not think the new actress "the greatest prodigy that ever appeared, nor go to see her act the same part every week and crying my eyes out every time. Were I five-and-twenty, I suppose I should weep myself blind, for she is a fine actress. . . ."[26] And, fifteen years later, an Exeter paper, reporting on her performance as Belvidera, in 1797, records that "when under the agonies of distress in the concluding scene she gave a loud shriek, it was immediately followed by a real hysteric fit in all of the fair and beautiful females who composed the audience."[27]

No one else had the same evocative powers as Mrs. Siddons and fainting fits became less frequent after her retirement. But there was no absence of tears in the early nineteenth-century theatre. At a performance of *The Wreck Ashore* at the Adelphi in 1837, "many were the eyes and voices that sympathized with the sorrows of Alice," wrote Charles Rice, "and numerous were the yards of cambric that bore witness to the sincerity of their feelings."[28] And Edward Fitzball reports of Mrs. West in *Jonathan Bradford* (1833) that her look of "pale maternal despair" as she uttered the words, "My children! My children! What will become of them?" were "a never-failing signal for universal tears." Fitzball claims to have seen the house dissolve into a "general burst of tears" over and over again at the end of *Azael, The Prodigal Son* (1851). "It *is* possible," he writes with the air of a master practitioner, "to dissolve a whole audience into tears, with only four words, *judiciously placed.*"[29]

In 1813, when the young William Macready produced *King John* at Newcastle, he "drilled the Prince Arthur by frequent rehearsals to cause abundant tears and hysterics in the boxes."[30] It must be many years now since a producer has positively striven to promote hysteria in his audience, and it is improbable that any theatre performance, however calculated, will ever produce such an effect again. A few may sometimes feel the moistened eyelash. Once in a way a trick of acting may surprise a man and betray him into emotion "because he cannot avoid it." But these things are nothing to compare with the normal behaviour of those simple hearts who regularly lamented with Mrs. Barry and Mrs. Porter, who swooned for Colman, or had hysterics at the bidding of Macready. In those days 'not a dry eye in the house' was a plain statement of fact.

The theatres of the eighteenth and the twentieth centuries are wide apart—but there is at least one place of common ground between them. We do produce Shakespeare. When Boswell went to see Garrick as Lear he kept himself "at a distance from all acquaintances, and got into a proper frame. Mr. Garrick gave me the most perfect satisfaction. I was fully moved, and I shed abundance of tears."[31] Hazlitt reported the same phenomenon; "the whole audience remained bathed in silent tears" during Garrick's acting of the part.[32] Who ever saw a whole audience in tears at a twentieth-century *King Lear*?

Perhaps the modern audience's frigidity is conveyed to it by the frigidity which reigns upon the stage. I have heard Ada Reeve say how the tears would stream down the cheeks of Henry Hampton in the days when she acted with him as a child in melodrama. No one wept for Belvidera at the recent London revival of *Venice Preserv'd*, which was largely because Belvidera did not weep for herself. Things were very different in 1764, when the Drury Lane prompter noted in his diary that "Mr. Powell played Lusignan with great Feeling but spoke much too low, and cryed too much."[33]

But they do cry (or appear to cry) on the films, and that is one of the reasons why an audience does not disdain to weep a little in the cinema. The wide liberties of the motion picture is another reason. At no time has a theatre playwright been able to show a close-up of a mother's smile, or a baby laughing through a jam-smudged face. He can not do these things, and now he no longer produces the kind of play which so cunningly ensnared our less experienced ancestors. We do not see tragedies like *Douglas*, the play which unhinged the two young ladies at Bath: we do not see melodramatic thrillers with ghosts and dungeons, lost heirs and insulted innocence; we do not see those romantic plays by W. G. Wills which gave such opportunities to Irving and Ellen Terry to draw the tears from Lyceum audiences. The nearest we have got to that sort of thing in this century has been the Grand Guignol—which incited fright, not the emotions of pity or grief.

It was in the age which invented gentility that public enthusiasm became unfashionable. The eighteenth century advertised a long list of offences involving the death penalty, but there was also an enormous area of behaviour in which no rules existed at all. Responsibilities were eagerly avoided. A delightful confusion prevailed. No one had ever heard of an inhibition. And no one—except

Lord Chesterfield—had ever suspected that it was un-English to betray emotion.

REFERENCES

1. Walpole, Feb. 4, 1742.
2. *Ibid.*, March 17, 1754.
3. *Ibid.*, Nov. 13, 1760.
4. *Ibid.*, Feb. 4, 1742.
5. *Ibid.*, May 12, 1791.
6. D'Arblay, *op. cit.*, vol. 1, p. 17; vol. 2, pp. 128, 172, 182, 256.
7. Hill, *op. cit.*, vol. 2, p. 333.
8. Macready, *op. cit.*, vol. 2, pp. 169-70.
9. Hill, *op. cit.*, vol. 1, p. 85.
10. Hill, *op. cit.*, vol. 1, p. 205.
11. Davies, *Dramatic Miscellanies*, 1784, vol. 3, p. 203.
12. Hill, *op. cit.*, vol. 1, p. 209.
13. Charke, *op. cit.*, pp. 197-8.
14. Davies, *Garrick*, vol. 1, pp. 142-3.
15. *Ibid.*, vol. 2, p. 182.
16. Benjamin Victor, *The History of the Theatres of London and Dublin*, 1761, vol. 1, p. 221.
17. D'Arblay, *op. cit.*, vol. 1, p. 385.
18. *The Life and Times of Frederick Reynolds*, 1826, vol. 1, pp. 295, 306.
19. Quoted by J. F. Bagster-Collins, *George Colman: the Younger*, 1946, p. 60.
20. Victor, *op. cit.*, vol. 1, pp. 55-6.
21. Hazlitt, *op. cit.*, p. 183.
22. Macready, *op. cit.*, vol. 1, p. 202.
23. *Ibid.*, p. 178.
24. Vol. 1, p. xli.
25. James Boaden, *Memoirs of Mrs. Siddons*, 1827, vol. 1, p. 327.
26. Walpole, Dec. 7, 1782. In 1793 even Walpole admitted shedding tears at young Bannister's performance in *The Children in the Wood*.
27. Quoted by Eric R. Delderfield, *Cavalcade by Candlelight, The Story of Exeter's Five Theatres 1735-1950* (1950), p. 37.
28. Rice, *op. cit.*, p. 31.
29. Fitzball, *op. cit.*, vol. 1, p. 248; vol. 2, pp. 275, 401.
30. Macready, *op. cit.*, vol. 1, p. 74.
31. *London Journal*, p. 257; May 12, 1763.
32. Hazlitt, *op. cit.*, p. 174. Hazlitt did not himself see Garrick. He claims to have "wept outright during the whole time" of Mrs. Siddons' performance as Isabella (*ibid.*, p. 199)—but he almost certainly referred to the tragic lady of *The Fatal Marriage*, not to the heroine of *Measure for Measure*.
33. MacMillan, *op. cit.*, p. 102.

IV

CONVERSATION IN THE THEATRE

"Ye beaux and belles, that form this splendid ring,
Suspend your conversation while I sing."
> From an Epilogue by Oliver
> Goldsmith, intended to be per-
> formed by Mrs. Bulkley and Miss
> Catley after *She Stoops to Conquer*

IV

"I HAVE often wished to live to see the day when prologues and epilogues should be no more. I wish a great genius would break through the silly, useless formality." So wrote Alexander Pope to Aaron Hill on September 12, 1738; and Hill replied on September 23:

"What you say against *Prologues* and *Epilogues*, is a truth, which I heartily feel and come into: but he ought to be very well *mounted* who is for leaping the hedges of custom. . . . And I doubt those disorderly heats, which must throw the *first* night into uproar, upon retrenching a popular folly, might have effects . . . to be apprehended."

Exactly the same point was made in a prologue written by Fielding a year or two later, in 1742. Garrick is supposed not to have had time to learn the lines and Macklin has bustled on as an embarrassed stop-gap. He explains the difficulty, and adds—

> I have been with the author, to know what's to be
>   done;
> For till the Prologue's spoke, Sir, says I, we can't go
>   on.
> "Pshaw! Rot the Prologue," says he, "then begin
>   without it."
> I told him 'twas impossible, you'd make such a rout
>   about it . . .

That apprehension lingered on for nearly a century, for when J. R. Planché proposed to omit the prologue

in 1824, Fawcett protested, "A five-act play, and no
prologue! They'll tear up the benches."[1] They did not
tear up the benches—but no one would have been
surprised if they had, for up to the middle of the nineteenth century a London theatre audience engaged in a
row on the smallest provocation. The audience of the
twentieth century is docile. It creeps into its seats at the
right time—or approximately at the right time—and it
listens, sometimes with enthusiasm, usually with respect,
always with fair manners, to whatever the players choose
to give them. The eighteenth-century audience had a
totally different idea of its own importance. As Garrick
admitted in Johnson's famous couplet:

> The drama's laws, the drama's patrons give,
> For we that live to please, must please to live.

There was a sadistic streak in those Georgian audiences.
The players were 'the servants of the public' in the most
bitter sense of the words. It would be more candid to
say that they were at the mercy of the public, utterly
dependent upon its favour.

In 1763 when the audience were smashing Drury Lane
as a protest against Garrick's new prices, the actor Moody
prevented one of the rioters from setting fire to the
theatre. This was regarded as a monstrous affront, and
the audience demanded that he should go down on his
knees and beg for pardon. Moody refused with an oath—
but "the tumult was so great," wrote Thomas Davies,
"that to appease their wrath, Mr. Garrick promised he
should not appear on the stage again during the time he
was under their displeasure."[2]

Tate Wilkinson has an interesting story about Kemble

at York in 1779 which ended more to the advantage of the actor.

A lady of family, well known in the county, was in the stage box. "She had her beaux to talk and laugh with," says Wilkinson, and unluckily she took a sudden dislike for the tragedy heroine, never failing on her appearance "to shew her great disapprobation, by the strongest marks of contempt and ridicule. From some unaccountable partiality, she had also adopted an opinion greatly to the prejudice of Mr. Kemble." In the last act this lady behaved so badly that Kemble suddenly stopped, and, when called on by the audience to go on, he "with great gravity, and a pointed bow to the stage box, said he was ready to proceed with the play as soon as *that* lady had finished her conversation. . . . This called up the roses into cheeks not the most remarkable for being feminine or delicate; and fury, indignation, and lightning flashed from her eyes: the audience were roused from their stupor, and in general hissed the lady in the stage box, and several voices cried *'Out! Out!'* " The lady's gentlemen friends hurried round to the manager and insisted on an explanation from the stage. But in the meantime the rest of the audience had laid their heads together, and when Kemble appeared to make his explanation he was greeted with cries of "No apology." Speak he did in explanation of what had occurred, but he utterly refused to ask pardon and left the stage amid bursts of approbation from the audience. Twice during the next fortnight the same party attempted to extract an apology and on each occasion Kemble obtained the loud support of the audience.[3]

It will be noticed that this disturbance arose in the first place out of the loud conversation of the lady in the stage box. The violent manners of the eighteenth-century theatre can be understood fairly easily. It is much more difficult to understand their *ordinary* manners. If they enjoyed the theatre why did they drop in at odd times? Above all, why did they come to talk?

The answer to this question is partly concerned with the architecture of the Georgian theatre. The eighteenth-century auditorium was hoop-shaped, and the boxes—in its final development—ran all round the circle. It made a pretty building and was excellent for sight and sound, for the stage still jutted out a short distance into the auditorium. Increasing needs of space have resulted in the theatre of today becoming more and more rectangular and less and less attractive, with the particular result that the boxes are usually facing the wrong way. But anyone who has ever sat in a box at the round-shaped Albert Hall will know the sense of comfort and privacy that a box can give—even though the seats are shared between several parties, as indeed they were in the Georgian theatre.

Undoubtedly the boxes promoted conversation, and apparently it was the smart thing to be heard as well as seen, for Colley Cibber, in *The Provoked Husband* (1728), makes Lady Townly say, "A married woman may have men at her toilet; invite them to dinner; appoint them a party in the stage box at the play; engross the conversation there; call them by their Christian names; talk louder than the players . . ." And Lord Dapper in Fielding's *The Historical Register for 1736* (1737), claims that "as I am one half of the play in the Green-room talking to the actresses, and the other half in the boxes talking to the women of quality, I have an opportunity of seeing something of the play, and perhaps may be as good a judge as another." In another of Fielding's plays, *Miss Lucy in Town* (1742), Tawdry declares that fine ladies arrive late on purpose, "make curtsies to their acquaintance, and then talk and laugh as loud as they are able."[4]

It was not only the Lady Townlys and Lord Dappers who talked. Fanny Burney, surely a lady of the most correct behaviour, was always ready for a cosy chat in a box at the theatre. At Bath in 1780 she declares how a friend "placed himself exactly behind me, but very quietly and silently, and did not, for some minutes, speak to me; afterwards, however, he did a little—except when my favourite, Mr. Lee, who acted Old Norval, in *Douglas*, was on the stage, and then he was strictly silent."

In 1788 Miss Burney was at Cheltenham with the Court as a keeper of the robes to Queen Charlotte. Mrs. Jordan was at the theatre playing Sir Harry Wildair, and although Fanny stiffly disapproved of the piece, she contrived none the less to enjoy a pleasant evening. "It is a very disagreeable play," she notes, "and wholly abounding in all that can do violence to innocence and morality: but it gave me an evening with that sweet young friend and we neither of us cared much for the stage while both had so much to communicate and to hear of nearer interest."

In the following year she seems to have passed an equally delightful evening with Lord Mountmorres at a Royal Command performance of *The Dramatist*. "We heard very ill," she writes complacently. "Missing the beginning we understood still worse: so that in the end I was indebted to my new associate for all the entertainment I received the whole evening."

A few years later Michael Kelly was at the playhouse

to see Dowton in *The Jew*. Without any sense of impropriety he records that he called out to a gentleman *"who was sitting within three boxes of our party"* [my italics] " 'this is fine acting; this, I'll answer for it, will do!' "[5]

It is clear that everybody talked in the boxes of the Georgian theatre. And conversation was not confined to the boxes. In 1783 Miss Burney was at the opera house with Mrs. and Miss Thrale. They sat in the pit, which was what we should now call the stalls. Pacchierotti, she notes, "was charmingly in voice, and we sat near the orchestra and I heard him to all possible advantage." Perhaps she heard less of the rest of the opera for she seems to have been in constant conversation with a gentleman who sat, not next, but next but one to her. "Mr. J—, though he talked to me very much, never did it while the Pac. was singing, or while anything else was going forward that was worth attention."

The most curious of Fanny Burney's references to conversation in public places concerns a visit to Westminster Abbey to hear a performance of Handel's *Messiah* on May 28, 1790. Dr. Burney was there, too, and, if words mean anything at all, it appears that they conversed together throughout the entire performance. "Chance favoured me," says she. "We found so little room, that we were fain to accept two vacant places at once, though they separated us from my uncle, Mr. Burney and his brother James, who were all there, and all meant to be of the same party. I might not, at another time, have rejoiced at this disunion, but it was now most opportune: it gave me three hours conference with my dearest father—the only conference of that length I have had in four years." After which she records what they said to each other, to the extent of two and a half pages

—but (not unnaturally in the circumstances) never a word about Handel.[6]

Much earlier in the century Mrs. Pendarves (afterwards the famous Mrs. Delany and a friend of the youthful Fanny Burney) found herself stumped at the opera by a very unexpected turn in the conversation, when Lord Baltimore confided that he had been in love with her for five years. "I was in such confusion," she writes, "I knew not what I saw or heard for some time, but finding he was going on with the same subject, I softly begged he would not interrupt my attention to the opera, as if he had anything to say to me, that was *not* the proper place."[7]

An eighteenth-century audience could not be commanded. Occasionally it could be led. James Boaden says that in Garrick's small theatre "conversation above a whisper was checked at once as indecent while so great a man was upon the stage; and the necessity of profound silence during certain scenes, introduced the custom of stationing what were called *hush* men, in different parts of the house, who . . . begot an awful attention in the audience and left the full impression of his vast powers upon the suspended and chilled spectators."[8] Evidently without such special organization the audience exchanged remarks throughout the whole evening. Sometimes, on occasions of exceptional excitement, the noise was overwhelming. On the night of December 1, 1804, when Master Betty made his first appearance at Covent Garden in *Barbarossa*, because his character, Achmet, did not appear until Act 2, the whole of the first act was ignored and the voices of the actors drowned by the continual murmuring and mounting excitement of the house.

Even the normal noises of the theatre were distracting.

F

Kemble complained that he never performed Lear as well as he rehearsed it. "An audience quite unsettled him; the noise of the box-doors caught his ear and routed all his meditated effects."[9] The noise of the box-doors: here is another peculiarity of the Georgian theatre. Patrons were inexplicably carefree about when they came in. Writing of his first sight of Garrick in 1744, Aaron Hill remarks that he intends to see him "quite through *Richard*" as though that were a most unusual compliment.[10] Nor was it only a matter of being late: they walked about and visited their friends in other boxes, treating the stage, whenever the interest flagged, with something of that modified attention that supper parties give to a cabaret show. Box-doors were normally kept shut, and every time anyone went in or out there must have been a clicking and a snapping over and above the sound of feet and dresses and whispered conversation. In the early Georgian theatre, when box money was collected inside the house, the "frisking in and out", as a contemporary put it, must have been continuous.

Garrick made the box-seats pay at the door, which diminished the confusion, but that people were still chattering in the theatre seventy years later is shown by Hazlitt, who gives a clear statement not only of what the actor had to contend against, but also of the trials of the serious lover of the drama in 1815. He is writing about the little Haymarket Theatre. "If, for example," he says, "a party of elderly gentlewomen should come into a box close at your elbow, and immediately begin to talk loud, with an evident disregard of those around them, your only chance is either to quit the house altogether, or (if you really wish to hear the play) to remove to the very opposite side of it; for the ill-breeding of persons of that class, sex, and time of life, is incorrigible. At the great theatres, it is sometimes very difficult to hear, for the noise and quarrelling in the gallery; here the only interruption to the performance is from the overflowing garrulity and friendly tittle-tattle of the boxes."[11]

A year after Hazlitt wrote that remonstrance, Miss Kelly, says Genest, was so interrupted in Lucy Lockit "by the perpetual talking of a party in the stage box that she made a pause, and gave a significant look—this not producing the desired effect, she, with a spirit much to be commended, made an appeal to the audience." Genest adds the grave comment, "This mode of interrupting the play by idle conversation may be very fashionable, but it is certainly very contrary to *real* politeness."[12] That same year, 1816, William Macready, who had come to Liverpool to meet his sailor brother, was watching a performance of *Guy Mannering*—"dividing my attention," he writes, "between the actors and the audience, when, to my surprise and great delight, three or four boxes off I saw my brother. I did not wait for the box-keeper's key, but somewhat indecorously I must confess, clambered over the intervening partitions to shake hands with him, which I did in a tumult of joy that attracted more observation than I desired. We sat out the piece together, to which however the mutual information we had to give allowed us to pay little attention."[13]

The word "attention" is the key to that story. If Macready had been attending to the play in the first place he would never have seen his brother. But he was looking at the audience as much as at the actors. Fanny Burney had used much the same language thirty years before. Her beau, she said, did not interrupt when anything was going forward "worth attention". A great part of the Georgian audience seems to have been incapable of attention. The Princess Charlotte "talked frequently and loudly" even during the private performance given by Charles Mathews before the Prince Regent at Carlton House.[14] And Harriet Martineau was deeply shocked by the behaviour of the young Queen at Covent Garden in 1837. "It was not pleasant to see her, when Macready's Lear was fixing all other hearts and eyes, chattering to the Lord Chamberlain, and laughing, with her shoulder turned to the stage."[15]

There was no team work in the Georgian theatre—no 'production' as we know it. The drama depended upon individual triumphs. The star system evolved in an age when the attention of an audience was dearly won. What with Aaron Hill dropping in late, and Fanny Burney chatting with her friends; what with Hazlitt changing his seat to avoid the ladies gossiping in the next door box; what with Lord Baltimore proposing marriage to Mrs. Pendarves, and young Macready climbing over the box walls; and what with the arguments and the quarrels in the more distant parts of the house, an actor had to be really remarkable to command attention at all.

In the twentieth century the only remnant of the barrage of noise which used to be discharged from the auditorium, is that carefully timed rattle of cups, and the low chatter of waitresses which is heard one minute before the fall of the first act curtain at a matinée. Conversation may powerfully compete with an orchestral overture, but during the action of the play, it is entirely quelled. The audience has lost its ancient authority in the theatre. In matters of procedure "the judicature of the pit" no longer exists, and the spirit of the audience has gone with its authority. In the twentieth century the drama's patrons have grown wonderfully meek.

REFERENCES

1. J. R. Planché, *Recollections and Reflections*, 1872, p. 42.

2. Davies, *Garrick*, vol. 2, p. 6.

3. Wilkinson, *The Wandering Patentee*, vol. 2, p. 19 ff. On Sept. 5, 1787, Michael Kelly suffered from the same chattering female at Wakefield. See *Reminiscences*, vol. 1, pp. 309-10.

4. In the Restoration Theatre the fashionables had been as likely to play cards as to watch the play. See Act IV, *A True Widow* by Thomas Shadwell: "A Pox on 't, Madam! what should we do at this damn'd Playhouse? Let's send for some Cards, and play at Langtrillo in the Box."

5. Kelly, *op. cit.*, vol. 2, p. 125.

6. D'Arblay *op. cit*: vol. 1, p. 385; vol. 4, p. 207; vol. 5, p. 75; vol. 2, p. 234; vol. 5, pp. 126-7.

7. *Autobiography and Letters of Mary Granville, Mrs. Delany*, ed. Lady Llanover, 1861, vol. 1, p. 240. Cf. Horace Walpole to Horace Mann, Nov. 23, 1741: "You can not imagine what an entertaining fourth act of the opera we had the other night. Lord Vane, in the middle of the pit, making love to my lady."

8. James Boaden, *Memoirs of Mrs. Siddons*, vol. 2, p. 377.

9. *Ibid.*, vol. 2, p. 276.

10. Hill, *op. cit.*, vol. 2, p. 234.

11. Hazlitt, *op. cit.*, vol. 8, p. 237.

12. Genest, vol. 9, p. 423.

13. Macready, *op. cit.*, vol. 1, p. 123.

14. Mathews, *op. cit.*, vol. 2, p. 247.

15. Harriet Martineau, *Autobiography*, 2nd edition, 1877, vol. 2, p. 119.

V

GOD SAVE THE QUEEN

Here's a health to King George, peace and glory attend
    him!
  He's merciful, pious; he's prudent and just;
Long life, and a race like himself, Heaven send him,
  And humble the foes to his crown in the dust.

Isaac Bickerstaffe: Finale to
The Recruiting Serjeant (1770)

V

ON GREAT occasions, when the national anthem is nobly played, a theatre audience can find that simple air extremely thrilling. But great occasions are rare occasions; and when, in ordinary theatres and cinemas, the orchestra, or more often an amplified gramophone record, blares out 'God save the Queen,' or more often the first half of it, the audience scrambles to its feet, respectfully indeed, but without much ceremony. 'God save the Queen' has become a fixture in the theatre, and is, naturally, received with no more excitement than the equally regular ceremony of lowering the fire curtain.

It had a very different importance in the Georgian theatre.

Dr. Percy Scholes is the leading authority on the national anthem. His pamphlet *God Save the King: its history and romance,* published in 1942, is a masterly inquisition into the obscure pedigrees both of the words and of the music. My essay is concerned, not with the derivations of the national anthem, but with its history in the theatre after that remarkable September 28, 1745, when 'God save our noble King', in very nearly the form in which we know it, was sung from the stage of Drury Lane by the gentlemen of the theatre and three soloists, Mrs. Cibber, John Beard, and Thomas Reinhold. Performed in the midst of the Jacobite rebellion, on the day that the actors of Drury Lane had asked leave to raise 200 men "in Defence of his Majesty's Person and

Government; in which the whole company of Players are willing to engage", the anthem was received with tremendous enthusiasm. That is understandable. What is mysterious is the fact that that enthusiasm should have lasted for so long, and have imposed a habit on the English people so firmly that a song of personal loyalty to the sovereign has been converted to a national hymn, indispensable upon all public occasions.

How did it happen?

In the first place the immediate dangers of the rebellion over, the dramatists and managers were prompt to make use of a certain winner; and if a national occasion were lacking, it was not beyond an author's ingenuity to invent a theatrical excuse. You might suppose, at first thought, that Nathaniel Lee's old tragedy, *The Massacre of Paris*, would hardly suggest an opportunity for performing the English national anthem. But you would be reckoning without that old windbag, Aaron Hill, to whom the occasion presented no difficulty at all. *The Massacre of Paris* reminded him of the natural shortcomings of the French, and the general superiority of the English—and that made it perfectly simple for him to end the epilogue written for Mrs. Pritchard with these noble lines:

> FIR'D, with this *foretaste* of my country's *zeal*,
> Verse is (*alone*) too faint, for what I *feel*!
> Help me, ye souls of MUSICK—come—and SING,
> Tune my touch'd heart's plain prayer—
> > *God save the King.*

At which point Mrs. Pritchard is instructed to wave her handkerchief as a signal for Mr. Beard and other singers to appear.

The epilogue is undated—but a reference to Admiral Vernon, who held the North Sea command in 1745 and was cashiered in 1746, makes it certain that it was written during the first few months of the enthusiasm for the loyal hymn.

Aaron Hill died in 1750. Not valuable as literature, the rarely seen volumes of his letters and poems contain a great deal of entertaining information about his world and particularly about the theatre, for which he wrote so many notable failures.[1]

Tucked away at the end of the second volume is a plan for an opera to be called HENGIST *and* HORSA. Or, *The Origin of* ENGLAND. At the end Merlin foretells to Hengist the events of futurity and informs him that "there shall, at last, after twice seven hundred years, of various fate, have roll'd themselves away, arise a family of kings, his descendants, to remove all cause of misery, and bless this kingdom to the end of time, with peace, arts, arms, and an undying harmony, and balance between power and liberty. . . .

"While he is speaking these last words, the back scene breaks away, and discovers in effigy (as lately done to a great perfection) the whole present Royal Family, surrounded above, with angels, smiling, and pointing thro' clouds; from the midst of which a beam of light shoots down, over the head of the king, in the centre.

"After this, something significant being said by every character, the chorus closes the opera, with a moral advice; not to distrust, or complain of our fortune, but trust heaven for events. In which case there will, at last, arise happiness, to overbalance all our misfortunes."

Hengist and Horsa, unhappily, was never written. Only the plan remains. It is undated, but from its position in the book and from the nature of its sentiments, it may be taken to belong to the same period, shortly after the '45 rebellion.[2]

This adulation of George II was something new in English life. It had taken a rebellion to make the Hanoverians popular. The point was that in 1745 the words 'God save the King' were significant words, not only for His Majesty, but for all those who had staked their fortunes on the Hanoverian succession.

Popular as the song was round about 1745, it was not until much later that 'God save the King' was ineradicably implanted in the hearts of the English. If George III had never been ill, if the French Revolution had not happened, if England had not been constantly at war with France, 'God save the King' might have sunk into the background as an occasional loyal song. There were other songs which had an equally popular tradition in the theatre. 'Britons Strike Home', for instance, and 'Rule Britannia', were frequently played by the orchestra. Most popular of all was 'The Roast Beef of Old England' from Fielding's *Grub Street Opera* and *Don Quixote in England*, a song which had been pointedly sung by the audience during their successful riot against the French players at the Haymarket Theatre in 1738. 'Roast Beef' was constantly called for at both theatres—before the play, after the play, or between the acts, particularly on a first night. Horace Walpole refers to it in a letter of 1743—". . . the singers of *Roast Beef* from between the acts at both theatres." And, twenty years later, the young Boswell noted, "As is usual on first nights, some of us called to the music to play 'Roast Beef'."[3]

"The King is good and amiable in everything he does,

and seems to have no view but of contenting all the world," wrote Horace Walpole, December 5, 1760, shortly after the accession of George III. And he noted that "the first night the King went to the play . . . the whole audience sung *God save the King* in chorus."[4] It was not a compliment often repeated. George promptly alienated the affections of his people by attempting personal government, and in particular by his persecution of John Wilkes, and before long Walpole was reporting to Lord Hertford that "when the King comes to a theatre . . . there is not a single applause."[5]

At that date, and for a long time afterwards, it was 'Roast Beef' which looked like becoming a theatrical institution: but twenty-five years later, at the time of George III's illness, 'God save the King' was to sweep all rival songs before it. George III, rising on the successes of William Pitt, had at length found his way into the affections of his people, and extraordinary indeed was the expression of their sympathy. New verses fitting to the melancholy occasion were sung everywhere.

> Remove disease and pain,
> His health restore again,
> Let us not sue in vain,
> God save the King.

So sang the company of players from the stage of the Exeter Theatre, supported by the entire audience, in January, 1789.[6] By the middle of February the King had recovered and now 'God save the King' continued in powerful popularity as a song of thanksgiving. There is a prologue in Thomas Bellamy's *Miscellanies* (1794) evidently written in 1789, for it is marked "spoken by a

Country Manager on the opening of a New Theatre. *Written immediately after the Recovery of the King.*" Feeble as they are, the last four lines are typical of sentiments which were being expressed in every theatre in the country.

Bell rings.

I'm call'd—Ye mighty gods support our cause,
And hail the rising curtain with applause.

Going out, returns to the music.

A word my masters, touch the trembling string,
And as it rises play—GOD SAVE THE KING.

In June, the king went on a visit of convalescence to Lyndhurst and Weymouth. Fanny Burney, who accompanied the royal party as keeper of the robes to the Queen, recorded in her Diary how, when the King went for an airing, "these good villagers" accompanied him and "continued singing ['God save the King'] during the whole walk, without any intermission, except to shout 'Huzza!' at the end of every stanza." On Sunday the loyal hymn was sung in church by the whole congregation—and "misplaced as this was in a church," writes Miss Burney, "its intent was so kind, loyal, and affectionate, that I believe there was not a dry eye amongst either singers or hearers."

Everyone has heard how, at Weymouth, the royal bathing machine was followed into the sea by another one containing fiddlers, who played 'God save the King' while his Majesty took his dip. Less well known is the agreeable fact that the loyal legend was written in golden letters on most of the bathing machines and that the bathing women displayed it on the girdles which encircled their sturdy waists.

Back in London in November, the royal family attended the theatre. "At the end of the farce," wrote Miss Burney, " 'God save the King' was most vociferously called for from all parts of the theatre, and all the singers of the theatre came on the stage to sing it, joined by the whole audience, who kept it up till the sovereign of his people's hearts left the house." "Kept it up" is an interesting phrase. It seems that once a loyal crowd began singing 'God save the King' they could go on repeating it indefinitely.[7]

'Roast Beef' was still holding its ground, or Anthony Pasquin would not have written in *The Eccentricities of John Edwin*, published in 1791, of "charming the tenants of the upper gallery in a Theatre by the exhilarating tune of the Roast Beef of Old England, or God save the King, with a chorus"[8]: but the grim tragedies which were being acted across the channel were soon to bring a new political significance to the second of the two songs. A man declared himself by his attitude to the loyal anthem—and this must be accepted as the principal reason for the extraordinary scenes which were to follow in the English theatres.

The prologue to *The Sicilian Romance* by Henry Siddons, produced at Covent Garden in 1794, contains these lines:

With joyful acclamations now they ring
And the grey veteran sits him down to sing
The Briton's noblest theme—God save the King.

Today there is something comic in this picture of an old gentleman settling himself down to enjoy a nice patriotic song. There was nothing comic about it in 1794.

Tate Wilkinson has a lot to tell of this matter in the last volume of his autobiography, published in 1795. In 1793, while his company was playing in Hull, he received a long and critical anonymous letter—opening with a request that he would "relieve the greater part of the audience . . . from the disturbance which takes place on almost every evening of performance, owing to persons in the upper gallery calling for the *popular* tune of 'God save the King ' ". Wilkinson's reply to this letter is a commentary upon the political importance of the anthem, and an exposure both of the tyranny of audiences and of the impotence of managements. If "the discerning part of the audience cannot bring the rude part to order," he writes, "it would be a fruitless and dangerous attempt of the manager . . . for instead of being taken as meant, to preserve peace, secret enemies would purposely put a wrong and dangerous construction." At York he had attempted to have the anthem after the farce—that is, at the end of the entertainment—"but it only tended to make it more violent, and worse and worse," he writes; and then comes this revealing observation—"the cause is the obliging others to hear the song, as it is natural to shew the love of power when aided with opportunity, whether Jacobin or Royalist. The surest remedy is patience; by degrees they will weary of what certainly is tiresome, and very inconvenient to the performers. . . ."

It was monstrously inconvenient to the performers, because, always on the look-out for a chance to exercise their authority, the audience sometimes called for 'God save the King' four or five times in the course of the

evening, and usually insisted on the actors coming
forward to sing it—no matter at what interruption to
the business of the stage: it might be between the acts of
the tragedy, or just before the farce, with the actors
obliged to appear in their comic costumes. On one
occasion Wilkinson angrily records the behaviour of a
drunk, who jumped on the stage and himself performed
'God save the King' during the playing of a principal
scene.[9]

Thomas Dibdin has a similar story to tell of 1797 in
quite a different part of the country. "Political party
at that time ran very high in Maidstone," he writes,
"and a fierce dispute, amounting almost to a tumult
occurred in the course of the evening, respecting an
encore of 'God save the King'." For some time the
performance was held up while members of the audience,
led by Lord Romney, made impassioned speeches on the
subject.[10]

The whole country was infected by the loyal fever.
People sang 'God save the King' at private dinner tables.
In Manchester the public houses hung notices in the bars
'No Jacobins admitted here', and some newspapers (as
Ryley notes in *The Itinerant*)[11] were taken in "merely for
the purpose of a conflagration, during which the loyal
circle danced round the flame to the joyous chorus of
'God save the King'."

Even the degree of warmth with which the loyal hymn
was performed was narrowly calculated. In 1795, at
Drury Lane, the popular comedian John Bannister was
accused, first, of hanging back, and then of singing
reluctantly and feebly. He wrote to *The True Briton*, the
paper which had pressed the charge, explaining that he
had been "dressed in character to exhibit the ridiculous

G

conceits of the Apothecary in *The Prize*. My feelings, at the moment, made me question the propriety of such a personage coming forward conspicuously to join in music so serious as to have been repeatedly called sacred." The paper accepted that as a reason for not coming forward, but declared that there could be no excuse for Bannister singing so languidly when, in consequence of the urgent and personal call of several gentlemen in the boxes, he had at last joined in the song.[12]

Five years later, as the king was entering his box at Drury Lane, a madman fired a pistol at him. As soon as the commotion had died down everyone sang 'God save the King', and at the end of the play the anthem was again demanded by the whole house. As the assembled company was singing, a paper was passed to Michael Kelly with a verse composed by Sheridan for the occasion.

> From every latent foe,
> From the assassin's blow,
>   God save the King!
> O'er him thine arm extend,
> For Britain's sake defend
> Our father, prince, and friend.
>   God save the King!

The stanza was repeated three times with "most rapturous approbation."[13]

'God save the King' remained in hysterical popularity until well into the nineteenth century. Stars of the opera in particular, were expected to sing it. In 1809, when engaged to appear at the new Covent Garden, Madame Catalani was taught, with great labour, to reproduce the words of 'God save the King' and 'Rule Britannia'.

The O.P. riots (for which her engagement was one of the excuses) prevented her performing the anthem then, but in 1811 she was singing it at the Opera House with Tramezzani, who electrified the house (so Macready recorded) "by the discrimination and energy with which he invoked the divine aid" in 'O Lord, our God, arise'. Hazlitt took quite a contrary view when he heard the same gentleman with Madam Grassini in 1814. The second verse, according to him, was torn to tatters "with every preposterous accompaniment of imitative action." Into

> Scatter his enemies
> And make them fall

Tramezzani "introduced as much heroic action, as if Jove, in the first line had had to shake a thousand thunderbolts from his hand, and in the next to transfix the giants to the earth. The bow with which this celebrated actor quitted the stage was endless and inimitable."

Madame Catalani was still singing 'God save the King' at Drury Lane in 1824, but she never succeeded in memorizing the words. Elliston's biography contains a grotesque version transcribed in Anglo-Italian phonetics and invariably used by the prima donna whenever called upon to perform the loyal hymn.[14]

"The surest remedy is patience," wrote poor exasperated old Wilkinson. "By degrees they will weary of what certainly is tiresome." It took these loyal tyrannical audiences many long years to do that, for the anthem could be used as a political argument upon almost any occasion. In 1796, shortly after the separation of the

Prince and Princess of Wales, the Princess was accorded
a great welcome at the Opera House, "and it was well
two other persons were not there," wrote Horace Walpole,
meaning the Prince and Lady Jersey, "as insults were
loudly declared to be intended, and on their not appearing, 'God save the *King*' was called for, and sung with
the same view."[15]

Twenty-five years later, when Queen Caroline visited
Drury Lane on May 14, 1821, the audience was backing
the other side in the long quarrel. As soon as they saw
the Queen, they insisted on 'God save the King' and it
was sung exactly in the manner condemned by Wilkinson
twenty-six years before, between the tragedy and the
farce, half the company dressed for *Malino Faliero* and
half for *Giovanni in London*—"a mixture of Demons and
Doges, Vixens and Venetians." And "dissociated as
were the characters," writes Elliston's biographer, "the
Anthem was equally discordant, and after considerable
uproar, which the greater part of the auditory appeared
especially to enjoy, the Queen retired and peace was
restored."[16]

The political significance of the song was diminished
by the cessation of the Napoleonic wars—but, if the people
did not offer the loyal supplication as fervently for George
IV as they had done for his father, the new king was
very ready to supply the deficiency. When George IV gave
a private picnic party at Virginia Water, he would have
himself welcomed with the strains of 'God save the King',
played by a band moored on the lake. Another curious
instance of a royal fondness for the song is reported in
a letter of Lady Lyttleton, written from Windsor Castle,
November 9, 1839. "The Cambridges are gone," she says,
"and the Castle is still as death, for want of the Duke . . .

He shouted on to the last, singing the quadrilles while they danced, and 'God save the Queen' while we dined, rather than be silent."[17]

With the accession of Victoria the loyal hymn became truly the national anthem. When the Queen and Prince Albert visited Covent Garden in 1840 there were no unseemly demands for 'God save the Queen'. Everything was arranged, and J. R. Planché was able to record, "the wonderful sight the house presented . . . as the curtain rose to the first bars of the National Anthem."[18]

On May 30, 1842, a madman fired at the Queen and Prince Albert as they drove down Constitution Hill. Next night they visited the opera. The anthem had already been sung and the opera begun when Her Majesty entered her box. The performance was immediately interrupted by an enthusiastic demonstration and "the opera was not suffered to proceed," says *The Times* report, "till the National Anthem was again sung." There were bursts of applause after almost every line, particularly after 'scatter her enemies' which "called forth the most deafening acclamations." This must have been one of the last occasions when the national anthem was sung with more than formal reference to the royal safety.

After the death of The Prince Consort many years were to pass before Victoria emerged from her seclusion. *More Leaves from a Journal of a Life in the Highlands,* 1884, reveals that the widowed Queen was often welcomed in Scotland with spontaneous performances of 'God save the Queen'; but it must have been during those years of her retirement that the loyal hymn declined into the more formal anthem that it is today.

'God save the King' was converted from a hymn of

personal loyalty to a national anthem by the pressure of politics and the tyrannical behaviour of theatre audiences. But it began in the theatre and it lives on in the theatre. And even now the air has only to be played well to assert its old authority. The house could hardly have been more moved on the night of September 28, 1745, than it was every night throughout the run of Noel Coward's *Cavalcade*, when 'God save the King' was sung by the entire cast from the stage of the same playhouse where (in the earlier building) Mrs. Cibber, John Beard, Thomas Reinhold, and the gentlemen of the theatre, first performed it over two hundred years ago.

REFERENCES

1. "Heavens preserve you!" wrote George Steevens to Garrick, Jan. 2, 1775 —adding on his own account, "and keep me from ever seeing more of *Zara* than the second act!" *The Private Correspondence of David Garrick*, vol. 2, p. 35.

2. Aaron Hill is something of a joke, but his remarkable generosity must not be unrecorded. He is said to have taken only one benefit, just before his death. The profits of *Zara* he gave to one friend, and of *Fatal Extravagance* to another. Some of his work he gave to the players free.

3. *London Journal*, pp. 152-5: Jan. 19, 1763.

4. Walpole, Nov. 24, 1760.

5. Dec. 29, 1763. Also, on the following Jan. 22: "the people . . . received the King and Queen without the least symptom of applause".

6. Quoted by Eric R. Delderfield, *op. cit.*, p. 37.

7. D'Arblay, *op. cit.*, vol. 5, pp. 30, 31, 33, 34, 76-7.

8. Anthony Pasquin, *The Eccentricities of John Edwin*, 1791, p. 56.

9. Wilkinson, *The Wandering Patentee*, vol. 4, pp. 109-10, 117-18, 163-4, 211.

10. Dibdin, *op. cit.*, vol. 1, p. 209.

11. Ryley, *op. cit.*, vol. 3, pp. 295-6.

12. John Adolphus, *Memoirs of John Bannister*, 1839, vol. 1, p. 357.

13. *Ibid.*, vol. 2, pp. 56-8.

14. Raymond, *op. cit.*, p. 344. The solo performance has not been unknown in the twentieth century. Clara Butt sang the anthem during the 1914 war. Eva Turner sang it on the stage of Covent Garden at King George V's Jubilee celebrations.

15. Walpole, May 30, 1796.

16. Raymond, *op. cit.*, p. 296.

17. *Correspondence of Sarah Spencer, Lady Lyttleton, 1787-1870*, ed. Mrs. Hugh Wyndham, 1912, p. 294.

18. Planché, *op. cit.*, p. 265.

VI

MR. VINCENT CRUMMLES

"Of provincial celebrity!!!"
Nicholas Nickleby

VI

OF ALL the comic characters of Charles Dickens there is none who is closer the truth than Mr. Vincent Crummles. Dickens commonly erred on the side of exaggeration. It was not possible for him to exaggerate Crummles. There is hardly an extravagance in *Nicholas Nickleby* which cannot be matched in the Georgian theatre, hardly a characteristic of the Georgian theatre which Dickens has not reproduced in *Nicholas Nickleby*. In the following notes I have compared fact with fiction, and endeavoured to show how the Dickensian and the Georgian theatres illuminate each other.*

Chapter Twenty-Two

1.

"A couple of boys, one of them very tall and the other very short, both dressed as sailors . . . fighting what is called in play-bills a terrific combat."

The combat between the Crummles boys in the characters of a short and a tall sailor is a comment on a familiar feature of the Georgian theatre. The Jolly Jack Tar (deriving principally from the novels of Smollett) had established himself on the English stage in the last half of the eighteenth century.[1] Early in the nineteenth century he had grown into a theatrical cliché, partly

* Four numbers of *The Dickensian*, 1949 and 1950, contain valuable notes on *Nicholas Nickleby* by Mr. T. W. Hill, commenting on obscure references and obsolete phrases, and resolving those problems of time and topography which even the best novelists leave behind them. Mr. Hill's notes and mine are of an entirely different character and hardly overlap at any point.

owing to the patriotic fervour promoted by the naval victories of the French wars, partly owing to the high moral part which the naval hero immediately assumed in the new and immensely popular entertainment of the melodrama. 'Virtue triumphant' was the motto of melodrama, and it could only be sufficiently triumphant if it were exposed to tremendous trials. It was, as Mr. Crummles well understood, "the essence of the combat" that there should be a disparity between the two sailors, both in size and in moral character—"unless," as he rightly added, "there's at least five to one." A rich example of this hero-outnumbered convention was advertised in *The Morning Chronicle*, September 19, 1791. A Grand Historical Entertainment at Astley's called *The Victorious Tars* contained "A GRAND AMBUSCADE and several combats between YOUNG ASTLEY (as an English Captain) and a Tribe of Savages."

Combats were often introduced between the pieces as separate displays (such as the act which the Crummles boys were rehearsing). Any which took place in the natural course of a drama were fought for all they were worth. Telling the story of his first appearance, in the part of Richmond, Charles Mathews confesses that he and Richard III (another beginner) prolonged the fight to such an extravagant length that the audience shouted with laughter.[2] Mr. Lenville's habit of fencing with his walking-stick was a playful reflection of the tragic combats in which he indulged at night.

2.

Mr. Crummles was proceeding to Portsmouth "(not for the regular season, but in the course of a wandering speculation) after fulfilling an engagement at Guildford with the greatest applause."

All the well established provincial companies moved in a small recognized circuit. Tate Wilkinson has given exact details of the movements of his company during the season 1791-2. Wakefield, September 2-26; Doncaster, September 27-October 29; Hull, November 1-February 3; York, February 7-May 16; Leeds, May 18-July 30; Pontefract, August 1-18; York, August 20-27; Leeds, August 29-September 4; Wakefield, September 5. Other famous provincial organizations were the Norwich circuit (which included Ipswich, Bury St. Edmunds, Colchester, King's Lynn, Yarmouth and Cambridge) and the Canterbury circuit travelled by Mrs. Baker's company.[3] That Mr. Crummles's company was no one-night, barn-storming affair, is proved by the fact that even on a "wandering speculation," he originally planned to play at Portsmouth for at least three weeks. In fact, owing to the great success of "Mr. Johnson," he stayed there for at least five. After Portsmouth the company were to play one week at Ryde, and thence proceed to Winchester.

Mr. James G. Ollé has pointed out in *The Dickensian* (June 1951) that following a disastrous year in 1836 there was no regular season at the Portsmouth theatre in 1837, though the Davenport company played there for some nights in March and April—when Miss Davenport, "the most celebrated Juvenile Actress of the day", appeared in a vast variety of songs, dances, and characters ranging from Little Pickle to Shylock. Dickens visited Portsmouth early in 1838 and, Mr. Ollé observes, "the sight of a weather-worn playbill clinging to the theatre's wall, advertising the Davenport season of the previous year, may be the simple explanation of the relationship between T. D. Davenport and his daughter Jean, and Vincent Crummles and his daughter, 'The Infant Phenomenon'." It may be: but Dickens had probably encountered Mr. and Mrs. Davenport some years before; in 1832 Davenport had been the manager of a little unlicensed theatre in Westminster. The important thing is not so much the connection between Crummles and Davenport as the unexpected accuracy of Dickens's information about the Portsmouth theatre. "Not for the regular season, but in the course of a wandering specu-lation" is an exact description of theatrical conditions in the unprosperous Portsmouth year of 1837.

3.
"Front Grooves O.P."

The scenery in the Georgian theatre was guided by a system of grooves attached both to the stage floor and to the fly-floor, holding the bottoms and the heads of the flats and wings.[4] Directed by these grooves the scenery slid on and off in full view of the audience. Compare a comment of Tate Wilkinson's on old stock scenery: "I never see these wings slide on but I feel as if seeing my very old acquaintance unexpectedly."[5] The grooves lasted till the 1880's. In 1875 Henry Irving could say in a speech, with full confidence of being understood: "The scene of [an actor's] life may shift from poverty to comfort almost as quickly as in the stage grooves the cottage gives place to the palace."[6]

The O.P. (opposite prompt) side was traditionally the side on the audience's left. Confusion often arises on this matter because, necessarily, the prompt side in a theatre is wherever the prompter's desk and stool happens to be, and sometimes the prompt side and the O.P. side are reversed—particularly in modern theatres where architecture and tradition are not always at one. See also page 120.

4.

"I had a dog that lived and died in [the profession] from a puppy; and my chaise pony goes on, in *Timour the Tartar*."

The reference to stage animals is not extravagant. It was a dog (he was trained to dive into a pool and rescue a child) that made the hit of the season in Frederick Reynolds's drama, *The Caravan* (Drury Lane, 1803). *Timour the Tartar* was full of animals and was one of the plays burlesqued by Colman in *The Quadrupeds of Quedlinburgh* (1811), an adaptation of the Frere-Canning burlesque, *The Rovers*.

5.

"Real Pump."

This admirable joke was anticipated, in part, by Ben Jonson. In the introduction to *Bartholomew Fair*, the stage-keeper complains bitterly of having been kicked around the tyring room by the author for suggesting some good stage effects. "Would not," he asks plaintively, "would not a fine pump upon the stage have done well for a property now? and a punk set under upon her head, with her stern upward, and have been soused by my witty young masters o' the Inns of Court?" Less to the point,

but worth recording, is the fact that Addison included a
tub in his comic list of effects to be auctioned at Covent
Garden (*Tatler*, July 16, 1709) ". . . a Rack, a Cart-
wheel, an Altar, a Helmet, a Back-Piece, a Brest-Plate, a
Bell, a Tub, and a Jointed-Baby."

6.

"A pound a week . . . and if we had a run of good
houses, nearly double the money."

Except that it included Smike's services and his
earnings as a writer, a pound a week is not so absurd as it
sounds. The top salary on the Norwich circuit at this
period was £1 15s. At the end of the eighteenth century
Tate Wilkinson had referred to Mr. Bucknall's salary as
"only sixteen shillings per week, and a benefit at York,
Hull, and Leeds, in yearly course, and those benefits
never more than *so so*."[7] When Henry Irving first went
on the stage, at Sunderland, in 1856, he received no pay
at all, during a lengthy trial period, after which, as
"walking gentleman", he was paid a weekly salary of
twenty-five shillings. In the following year, as juvenile
lead at Edinburgh his salary was only thirty shillings.

It is not clear on what principle Nicholas's salary was
fixed. At the end of the week in which his melodrama
was produced he received thirty shillings. The phrase
'if we had a run of good houses' suggests a sharing
arrangement, but the Crummles company was above
that. Besides, mention is made at the beginning of
Chapter 30 of Nicholas's "regular salary". The extra ten
shillings must have been payment for the play. No doubt,
as Nicholas was new to the business, the manager took
some small advantage of him.

7. The Stage Prince. *From a woodcut by George Cruikshank.*

THEATRE ROYAL
NORWICH-
Lessee and Manager - - - Mr. W. SIDNEY

MISS
M. SMITH
AND
MISS E. SMITH

Have the honor of announcing to their Friends and the Public, their

BENEFIT
Will take place on
MONDAY, MARCH 6TH.
Upon which occasion only
MR. & MRS. G. SMITH

will have the pleasure of re-appearing, after an absence of many years.

The Performances will Commence with Shakspeare's Play of

HAMLET
PRINCE OF DENMARK.

Hamlet, [by desire]		MISS MARY SMITH	
The Ghost - -		MR. GEO. SMITH	
Claudius	Mr. W. LOWE	Laertes	Mr. H. B. CROUCH
	Mr. MORGAN	Guildenstern	Miss L. DESMONDE
Polonius	Mr. E. STANLEY	Mr. ATKINS	Mr. MEANY
Rosencrantz	1st Actor	2nd Actor	
First Gravedigger -		- Mr. W. SIDNEY	
Second Gravedigger	Mr. ARTHUR WILLIAMS	Marcellus	Mr. WILSON
Horatio	Mr. G. NEWTON	Bernardo	Priest Mr. BROWN
		Mr. WILTON	
The Queen - -		MRS. GEO. SMITH	
Ophelia - -		MISS E. McDONNELL	
	Actress	Miss M. DESMONDE	

8. Part of Norwich Play-bill, 1865.

Chapter Twenty-Three

1.

"Wherein the names of Mr. Vincent Crummles, Mrs. Vincent Crummles, Master Crummles, Master P. Crummles, and Miss Crummles, were printed in very large letters, and everything else in very small ones."

Anyone acquainted with old play-bills will recognize this account. Part of a Norwich bill is produced below, announcing the exhibition of Miss Smith, and by desire too, in the part of Hamlet. Its date is 1865, some thirty years later than Crummles's period, but it still shows that confident determination of old time stage families to force themselves upon the public *en bloc*. Typographically it displays a skill nearly equal to that of Mrs. Grudden, "who had quite a genius for making out bills, being a great hand at throwing in the notes of admiration, and knowing from long experience exactly where the largest capitals ought to go."

This bill is chiefly devoted to the glory of the Smith family, still acting at Norwich, though the theatre was no longer under their management. It will be noticed that the Ghost (played by Mr. Geo. Smith) is announced in large type, while Claudius, Polonius, and Laertes are reckoned of no more account than the priest and the second grave-digger. Mr. Sidney, the largely proclaimed First Grave-digger, was the manager. He appears in capitals on all Norwich bills of the period.

2.

"Mrs. Vincent Crummles."

The queenly manner of Mrs. Crummles is curiously paralleled by that of the actress Hannah Brand, who was

for a time a member of the York company, and of whom
Tate Wilkinson wrote that "she only wanted a spear and
shield, to have awed the wondering beholders with her
grand and majestic portly bearing." In another place
Wilkinson very nearly uses Dickens's adjective of the
"charnel-house voice". "One day rapping at my door,
'Who's there,' says I, to which she replied as awfully as
the Ghost in *Hamlet*, 'It is Hannah Brand'."[8]

3.

"The Indian Savage and the Maiden."

The noble savage had been a popular figure on the
English stage for some time.[9] *Ko and Zoa; or The Belle
Sauvage* was produced at Sadler's Wells in 1802:
Pocahontas; or The Indian Princess at Drury Lane in 1820:
The Wigwam; or The Red Men of the Wilderness (dramatized
from Fenimore Cooper's *The Pioneers*) at Covent Garden
in 1830. 'The Indian Savage and the Maiden' was the
dregs of the Pocahontas story, with the sexes reversed.

4.

"The Infant Phenomenon."

Child actors had long been known in the theatre.Tom
Thumb, for instance, was always played by a child. Miss
Hinde (1754) and Master Hinde (1756) were aged five
when they played the part with the Norwich company.[10]
The child actor was transmogrified into the Infant
Phenomenon when he rejected diminutive parts like Tom
Thumb and the little princes in *Richard III*, and presumed
to appear as an adult. The most famous phenomenon was
Master Betty, "the young Roscius", who appeared at
Covent Garden in 1804 and for a time achieved an

astounding success.[11] A horde of juvenile prodigies
followed in his wake, including Master Wigley, a child of
four and a half, who was advertised at Drury Lane to
"perform several pieces of military music on the bugle
horn" on June 17, 1805. The town put up with these
extraordinary little creatures for a long time. There is a
print dated 1824, of Master Grossmith of Reading, "as
he appeared at the London Theatres in the sixth year of
his age . . . in the character of Richard III."

In the provinces infant prodigies lingered even longer.
Miss Davenport (born 1829), supposed to be the found-
ation for Ninetta Crummles, played Shylock, Richard III,
Sir Peter Teazle, and other equally unsuitable parts, at
the age of eight. Many years later, Vesta Tilley was five
years old when she made her debut as a male impersonator
("The Pocket Sims Reeves") at Birmingham. See also
page 126.

5.

"Five people and a baby in the pit, and two boys in
the gallery."

As Mr. and Mrs. Crummles agreed, over the mutton
and onion sauce, provincial people were not very theatric-
ally minded. Most of the records of small travelling
companies are records of failure. Wilkinson recalls the
curtain rising at Harrogate with only one person in the
theatre. One night, at Wakefield, Lewis refused to play
because the house held only thirty shillings.[12] Pierce
Egan visited the Guildford theatre on election night
and found it empty except for "three little country boys
in the gallery."[13]

H

6.

"Mr. Lenville who does our first tragedy."

There was a strictly labelled hierarchy in the Georgian theatre, especially in the provinces, and no doubt about the credit and position of every actor in the company. The Norwich list included the following: 1st Tragedian, 1st Light Comedian, Heavy Man, 1st Low Comedian, 2nd Low Comedian, 1st Singing Man, 2nd Singing Man, 1st Old Man, 2nd Old Man, Walking Gentleman, 1st Tragedy Lady, 1st Comedy Lady, 1st Singing Lady, 2nd Singing Lady, Chambermaid and Dancer, Old Woman, Walking Lady, Utility, 2nd Utility.

At the general muster of the Crummles company all these types are clearly recognizable. 1st Tragedy, Mr. Lenville; 1st Light Comedian, the unnamed actor in the rough great-coat; 1st Low Comedian, Mr. Folair; 2nd Low Comedian, "the comic country man"; 1st Singing Man, the "slim young gentleman with weak eyes". The two old men were there and even the Walking Gentleman and the Utilities are found chatting together in a corner. Only the Heavy Man is missing. Perhaps he was ill that day. He certainly existed, for in Chapter 30 Mr. Folair refers to "Old Fluggers, who does the heavy business." In addition there was Mr. Crummles himself, who alternated, no doubt, between Tragedian and Heavy Man.

Mr. Crummles's claim to have played "the heavy children" when he was eighteen months old (chapter 22) is one of the very few pieces of exuberance in The Crummles picture. That the actor should have appeared at eighteen months is easily acceptable, but the "heavy children" is a Dickensian myth.

Probably the Crummles list would have included Mrs. Crummles as Heavy Woman, a term which referred not to the gravity of the actress herself but to the gravity of the parts which she played. This would have allowed for Miss Snevellicci as 1st Tragedy Lady (we know that she played Lady Macbeth) and Miss Ledrook as 1st Comedy Lady (Miss Snevellicci would never have been great friends with an inferior member of the company). With Mrs. Grudden clearly marked as Old Woman, Miss Belvawney ("who seldom aspired to speaking parts") as Utility, and the Phenomenon as dancer (she also played parts and did not confine herself to Chambermaids), it is evident that Miss Bravassa and Mrs. Lenville must have been the Singing Ladies, and Miss Gazingi the Walking Lady. It is true that Miss Bravassa was cast for a comedy role in the drama which Nicholas witnessed on his first night at Portsmouth, but on that evening, five weeks later, when the London manager was perceived in the boxes, Miss Bravassa had a song to sing, and no other lady is mentioned as singing. Besides, the Singing Ladies normally were comedy actresses.

The Singing Ladies and Gentlemen were important members of any provincial company, because the Georgian theatre had always to be equal to a burletta or comic opera. It was essential that a company should have sufficient talent to support *Thomas and Sally*, *Love in a Village*, or *Tom Thumb*.

There was not a wide difference of salaries in the company. In the Norwich company the tragedian got £1 15s. and the Utility £1 5s. But there would have been a very great difference between the benefits of the two actors: indeed the utility actor would certainly have had to share a benefit with some of his inferior colleagues.

The Norwich accounts show that benefits ranged between £160 and £46.

7.
"Old Bricks and Mortar."

Among the imperfections of the old style actor, Ryley lists "stamping before he made his appearance, crossing at every period, protruding the elbow, slapping the thigh, pointing the toe."[14]

8.
"Lengths; Quick Study."

Cant phrases of the stage. See pages 119, 186*f*.

9.
"Who could do anything from a dance to Lady Macbeth."

Such versatility was characteristic of Miss Snevellicci's period. Mrs. Jordan liked to try her hand at tragedy, and Mrs. Siddons attempted comedy. Actors sometimes rejected their parts after hearing the play read, but, on the whole, their anxiety, like Bottom's, was to play everything. In a provincial company they had every opportunity.

10.
"Knee-Smalls."

The playing of male leads by well-built actresses was a famous speciality of the Georgian theatre. Miss Snevellicci did not adopt tights at her benefit only. She wore them on the night when Nicholas first visited the

Portsmouth theatre, and she was wearing them on the night on which he announced his unexpected departure. When Nicholas called at Miss Snevellicci's rooms (chapter 24) he saw in a corner "the diminutive pair of top-boots in which Miss Snevellicci was accustomed to enact the little jockey." *The Little Jockey* was a farce produced at the Olympic Theatre on January 3, 1831—a date which fixes the Crummles company with certainty in the eighteen-thirties. See "Breeches Parts," page 160, and "Traditions of the Pantomime," pages 218*f.*

11.
"Retired up."

Dickens is using the language of the stage direction. Miss Snevellicci retired towards the back of the stage, or 'up-stage'.

12.
"Everybody for the procession."

Processions were greatly esteemed in the Georgian theatre. Tate Wilkinson, while visiting London in 1792, recorded that "the procession in *Cymon* was superior to anything of the kind I had ever witnessed." Other famous processions were those in *Papal Tyranny*, *Romeo and Juliet*, *Coriolanus*, *Henry VIII*, and Garrick's Shakespeare Jubilee. George IV's coronation in 1821 was the signal for a magnificent procession at Covent Garden in *Henry IV*, Part 2. The traditional march down at the end of the pantomime is the last vestige of this once familiar display.

13.

"Intrigue and Ways and Means you're all up in, so we shall only want one rehearsal."

Only new pieces were seriously rehearsed. The stock pieces were so well known that any actor could fill a part at one rehearsal in any company. It is strange that this stagnation should have settled equally on the London stage. When the provincial actor, Ryley, was given his chance at Drury Lane as Sir Peter Teazle, he was only allowed one rehearsal, "and what was my surprise and agitation, and alarm, when I found the manuscript from which this comedy was performed in provincial theatres, differed so materially from the original, it was utterly impossible to connect the speeches." This was Friday. The performance was Monday. He had to re-learn the part over the week-end and then, without further rehearsal, to make his *first* London appearance.[15]

14.

"Just turn that into English, and put your name on the title-page."

No proper system existed for protecting the author. Once a play was printed it was acted anywhere with impunity. To safeguard copyright as long as possible managers never allowed any actor a full copy of the play. Country managers sometimes attempted to take down a copy while a play was being acted, or even sat through several performances in an attempt to learn it by heart. Thomas Snagg and four friends transcribed *The School for Scandal* by sitting together in the gallery for four or five nights—a sufficient explanation of that provincial version of the play which so discomposed the unfortunate Ryley.[16] Many plays were lifted from the French. Thomas Holcroft went to Paris, witnessed *The Marriage of Figaro* every day for a week or ten days, learnt it by heart with the assistance of a friend, wrote it down, and from this translated the play for Covent Garden.[17]

15.
"You shall study Romeo."

There was nothing remarkable in Nicholas making a first appearance in a principal role. Stage aspirants commonly did make their debut in a leading part. It was up to them to show what they could do. See pages 11, 24. Eventually he made his first appearance as juvenile lead in the melodrama.

16.
"Rover".

Rover was the leading part in O'Keefe's *Wild Oats*. It was one of Elliston's favourite parts and would have been much prized by all actors in the "First Comedy" line. The gentleman "in a rough great-coat" would certainly have been in possession of the character in the Crummles company and would have had far more reason for quarrelling with Nicholas than Mr. Lenville had.

17.
"Here they are, cues and all."

The "number of little books," which Mr. Crummles thrust into Nicholas's hands, were "lengths". They contained, not the whole play, but only the speeches of one

part, with the cues. Parts are still distributed in this form
to small-part players.

Chapter Twenty-Four

1.

"And you close in with a picture."

"Close in" because of the drawing of the flats; "with
a picture", meaning the final pathetic tableau of the dis-
tressed lady fainting in the arms of the attached servant
while the little child kneels by her side holding her hand.
The flats closed in front of the tableau, thus ending one
scene and setting the stage for the next in a single motion.

The flats drew across at different points on the stage,
making a deep scene, a medium, or a shallow one as
desired. The medium size would have been needed for the
pas-de-deux; the following scene, therefore, would necessarily have been a shallow set—"a corridor" or "a street".

A letter from Mrs. Cibber to Garrick, December 11,
1746, gives another example of "closing-in", and for a
different reason. The stage at Drury Lane had been
"built up", to accommodate spectators, according to the
custom of the time at benefits.[18] But "as nobody came
there," writes Mrs. Cibber, "he shut in a flat scene to
hide it."[19]

2.

"She always sustained one, and not uncommonly
two or three, characters, every night."

This is no exaggeration of ordinary provincial practice,
as any theatre bill of the period will demonstrate. See
also pages 126, 137.

3.

"Which process . . . was put a stop to by another jerk of the bell."

Nowadays signals are given by lights, or very low buzzers. In the Georgian theatre orders had to be conveyed by audible signals, and the audience must have been perfectly acquainted with the bells which tinkled in the orchestra to start and stop the music, and the whistles which were blown for the changes of scenery.

Music always held an important place in the theatre. In the Restoration playhouse the performance was regularly preceded by three pieces of music known as the first, second and third music—an arrangement advertised in a play-bill of 1734 as follows: "Three PIECES will be performed before the PLAY begins. The first at five o'clock, the second at half-an-hour after five, and the third at six; at the end of which, the curtain will be drawn up."[20] Davies used the phrase in 1780 in his *Life of David Garrick* when he remarked on Dexter conversing with his friends in the pit, on the first night of his performing, "till the second music, which is generally played about half an hour before the curtain is drawn up, put him in mind that it was time to think of the stage apparatus."[21]

After the passing of the Licensing Act of 1737, music assumed a particular significance for certain people of the theatre. Strictly speaking, plays were only permitted in buildings which possessed a licence, and in London the patentees of the great theatres defended their rights vigorously. In the country it was easier to evade regulations, and the accepted device was to invite the public

The Stage Assassin.
From a woodcut by George Cruikshank.

to buy tickets for a concert of music, the play being supposed to be thrown in free. It was for this reason that the Norwich theatre between 1759 and 1768 was known as The Grand Concert Hall. In 1768, when the manager received a patent, he was able to call his house The Theatre Royal.[22] When Tate Wilkinson got a patent for his theatre at York he remarked on his troop "being relieved from the subterfuge of acting under a concert of music and presenting a play gratis."[23] The subterfuge

The Stage Assassin.
From a woodcut by George Cruikshank.

had been used even in London. "Between the parts of the
Concert will be presented *gratis* a Comedy, called the
Stratagem," is the advertisement for Goodman's Fields
on October 13, 1740; and the entertainment at which
Garrick made his first London appearance was billed as
"*A Concert of Vocal and Instrumental Music,* divided into
two parts."

The Portsmouth theatre would have been under no
necessity of providing a bogus concert of music in the

Crummles period, but the musical tradition was firmly established and there would have been no thought of beginning the play without a rouser in the way of an overture. A playhouse without an orchestra was, indeed, unheard of until the twentieth century, when union rates of pay enforced economies.

4.
"Miss Bravassa in all the sweetness of Miss Snevellicci's confidential friend."

The confidential friend, an essential figure of eighteenth-century tragedy, had been burlesqued in *The Critic* in 1779.

5.
"The plot was most interesting."

Of the three plays named by Mr. Crummles *Intrigue* and *Way and Means* are real plays, and not remotely like this one. Plays were commonly rehearsed and acted on the same day, and the fact that *The Mortal Struggle* was called for ten o'clock makes it almost certain that that was the play which Nicholas witnessed. It is typical of Dickens's fecundity that he should have described, in successive chapters, two entirely different kinds of drama. *The Mortal Struggle* was one of the old-fashioned "tale of terror" type. The play Nicholas was translating was an up-to-date melodrama.

6.
"Bespeak."

Miss Snevellicci's benefit was not strictly a bespeak, for, as she very soon found out, it was impossible to meet the requests of all her patrons. A bespeak and a benefit could only be interchangeable words when some sufficiently important patrons settled the matter for all. Horace Walpole (February 18, 1742) mentions that the Prince of Wales had purposely bespoken *The Unhappy Favourite* for Mrs. Porter's benefit in the hope that certain passages might be taken with an anti-Walpole significance. Mrs. Porter would hardly have cared what her other patrons wanted if she were going to be honoured by the Prince and his party. In its exact meaning a bespeak was a performance desired by some influential person or corporation. It benefited the management, but it was not a 'benefit'. See also "Bespeak", page 155.

7.

"A little canvassing takes place on these occasions."

There were those who remembered Mrs. Siddons in her provincial days, going from house to house and popping play-bills in the letterboxes. The personal appeal for support was a humiliating experience for the actor and a fine opportunity for condescension among patrons. See also page 152.

8.

"They were to have two-thirds of the profits by solemn treaty of agreement."

Two-thirds was the share exacted by Mrs. Baker of the Canterbury circuit. She and Crummles were less generous than Tate Wilkinson and James and George Smith, both of whom went equal shares with their actors above an agreed expenses fee. See "Benefit", page 149*f*.

9.

"Four shillings a-piece to the boxes."

Prices varied in different places but four shillings was a normal price at the opening of the nineteenth century. Mrs. Baker charged four shillings at Tunbridge Wells, three shillings in her other theatres. In London box seats were six, later seven, shillings—at minor theatres four.

10.

"Such fits of crying."

See "Not a Dry Eye in the House," pages 61*f*.

11.

"It included among other trifles, four pieces, divers songs, a few combats and several dances."

An exaggeration, which legitimately achieves its purpose of drawing attention to the monstrous medlies that filled the theatrical bills of some of the provincial theatres on benefit nights. By a happy chance Tate Wilkinson (who disapproved of such mixtures) has recorded the play-bill of Mrs. Davies's benefit which took place in Mr. Crummles's Portsmouth theatre in 1791. It included *The Brothers*; *The Author*; and Act 3 scene 1 of *Richard III* (with the two princes played by Miss Louisa Davies and Master William Davies—an infant pheno- menon of exceptional precocity, for he was only four years old). Between the acts of *The Brothers*, and at the end of the play, songs were sung by Miss Davies. This bill is not far short of Miss Snevellicci's.[24]

It is an uncommonly interesting fact that Mrs. Davies was the wife of the manager, and that Miss Davies, Miss Louisa Davies, and Master William Davies make up a family of exactly the same size as the Crummles party, with the sexes reversed. Crummles is supposed to have been founded on T. D. Davenport (1792–1851).[25] But authors build their characters from a multiplicity of materials, and Dickens may well have known Tate Wilkinson's two books of reminiscence.

12.

"At half-past five, there was a rush of four people to the gallery door; at a quarter before six, there were at least a dozen; at six o'clock the kicks were terrific; and when the elder Master Crummles opened the door, he was obliged to run behind it for his life. Fifteen shillings were taken by Mrs. Grudden in the first ten minutes."

This is an ironical reference to a common experience. Due no doubt to the ever present apprehension of offending the patrons, the front of the house organization in the Georgian theatre was deplorable. Normally the problem was how to entice people into the theatre—but on special occasions the problem was almost how to keep them out, or at least how to regulate their entry. People often crowded so closely past the pay-desk that the money could not be taken even from those who intended to pay. So many people entered without paying at one of Elliston's benefits that he had a plate passed round in the hope of recovering what he had lost. Banti and Michael Kelly suffered the same misfortune.

At a country performance for the benefit of Edward Everard the doors were opened before anyone was in position to take the money. The unhappy actor advertised an appeal for payment in the newspapers.

When George III and the King of Denmark attended Drury Lane in 1768, "the flood of people bore all before it," wrote Thomas Snagg, "and so many were jammed within the pit, boxes, and gallery that several overheated and fainting were only to be removed by ladders from the pit across the stage, and with infinite difficulty from the galleries and boxes."[26]

On the famous occasion of the opening performance of young Betty at Covent Garden, many people paid the price of box admission in order to get quickly inside the theatre. They then jumped from the boxes into the pit, thus securing places ahead of the more slowly moving pit queue; and when there was no possibility of the pit containing another person, the intruders sat down in the box seats which had already been reserved by other people. The audience was dishonest, but a management which knowingly admitted to the boxes more persons than the boxes would hold, was both dishonest and cowardly. The plain fact is that the proprietors of the Georgian theatre were afraid of the audience. It was not merely the drama's laws that the drama's patrons gave, it was all the laws for the conduct of the theatre.

13.
"There was a round of applause every time he spoke."

In the Georgian theatre the audience applauded individual speeches and popular sentiments. See page 43*f*.

14.
   "Blue Fire."

An essential effect in all the best melodramas. Recipes
for Blue Fire are recorded in the Theatrical notebooks of
T. H. Wilson Manley, preserved at the British Museum
(Add. MSS. 41,073-4).

15.
   "The audience (who had by this time increased
   considerably)."

Unpunctuality was one of the peculiarities of the
Georgian theatre. The practice in many theatres of
taking half-price after the third act of the play, had
something to do with it—but it does not explain more
than half of the problem. The fact was that people had
not learned to enjoy the drama for its own sake alone.
So long as they equally enjoyed talking and walking about
and quarrelling and hissing the play, they were likely to
drop in when it suited them and not when it suited the
actors. Even Queen Victoria, at the beginning of her
reign, made no attempt to be polite to the players.
"The Queen came in just after the beginning of the fourth
act," Macready noted in 1838.

16.
   "When Miss Snevellicci was called for at the end of
   the play."

No curtain call was mentioned at the end of the melodrama witnessed by Nicholas on the opening night. In the
1830's the custom was still not absolutely established.[27]
   I

Chapter Twenty-Five

1.

"The evenings when the theatre was closed, were reduced from three to two a week."

It was normal in the provinces to play only on certain nights of the week—except when business was peculiarly good. Until George Smith introduced nightly performances in 1842 the Norwich theatre (except in Race week) had been open on Monday, Wednesday, Thursday and Saturday.

Nor was it customary, in London, for actors to appear at every performance in the week. The plays alternated, and so did the casts. "Permit me to advise you to resolve not to act upon any Account above 3 times a Week," wrote a correspondent to Garrick, dismayed by the fact that he had performed in *Tancred* for nine nights. "Consider the part and whether Nature can well support the frequent Repetition of such Shocks."[28] "In London two nights a week were enough," said George Frederick Cooke, "at three I grumbled; four I would not do. I complained to Mr. Harris of playing four nights a week; I said 'it's too much sir'. 'Why yes,' says he, 'it's almost as much as playing six nights in the country at race week.' There he had me."[29] To the end of his career, in the middle of the nineteenth century, Macready was still contracting for so many nights a week.

2.

"She played Juliet and Helen MacGregor, and did the skipping-rope hornpipe between the pieces."

Helen MacGregor was a character in *Rob Roy*, a drama-

tization of Scott's novel by J. Pocock, produced at
Covent Garden in 1818.

To play in both pieces was quite ordinary, and Mrs.
Crummles's triple achievement was not impossible.
Dickens goes far when he suggests that a woman of Mrs.
Crummles's proportions could reasonably have played
Juliet at her last benefit—but, as in the matter of Miss
Snevellicci's play-bill, the exaggeration is only a little
beyond the sort of thing that actresses have done often
enough. That Mrs. Crummles, in her youth, should have
stood on her head on the butt end of a spear, surrounded
with blazing fireworks, is entirely credible.

3.

"Nicholas had the honour of playing in a slight piece
with Miss Petowker that night."

Presumably Nicholas was already acquainted with his
part, for he can only have had one rehearsal with Miss
Petowker. This was quite normal. Macready had no
more when he played with Mrs. Siddons in 1811.

4.

"The warmth of her reception was mainly attributable
to a most persevering umbrella in the upper boxes."

The great thing in the Georgian theatre was to make
as much noise as possible. Stumping on the floor with
stick or umbrella was one accepted method. Kicking the
panels of the boxes was another, and is recorded at the
end of Chapter 24 in the account of Miss Snevellicci's
benefit. "The tailor and his family kicked at the panels

of the upper boxes till they threatened to come out altogether." This sort of behaviour was presumably the origin of "bring the house down", a phrase duly incorporated by Dickens in Chapter 22.

5.

"Once he thought that a peculiarly shaped hat in the same corner was not wholly unknown to him."

Men wore hats inside the theatre till a surprisingly late date. See page 15, and the picture by Theodore Lane opposite page 144. Nicholas would hardly have been able to see as far as the upper boxes against the glare of modern stage lighting. In the Georgian theatre it was far easier to view the audience, and correspondingly more difficult to ignore them.

6.

"Mrs. Crummles advancing with that stage walk which consists of a stride and a stop alternately."

Mr. Felix Aylmer has pointed out that this stately mode of progression still survives on the continental opera stages.[30] Besides the actress's determination to appear regal, this walk was probably promoted originally by two practical considerations, the weight of the queenly train, and the rake of the Georgian stage. The writer of this note has walked upon what was one of the last of the unaltered Georgian stages—that of the Barnwell theatre, Cambridge, reconstructed in 1926–7 to make the Festival Theatre. The steepness of the rake was unexpected, and it was immediately clear that in the down-hill direction, a disciplined step was essential to dignity.

Chapter Twenty-Nine

1.

"A benefit was considered by the manager a very promising speculation."

By the manager, because the manager, according to normal provincial procedure, was a sharer in the profits. If Nicholas's terms were the same as Miss Snevellicci's, Mr. Crummles would have netted £40 to Nicholas's £20. See also pages 125, 149*f*.

2.

"Nicholas personated a vast variety of characters with undiminished success."

He must have been a remarkably quick study—but all the theatre bills bear witness to the fact that a provincial actor did play a bewildering number of parts. Henderson told Garrick (November 4, 1774) that, in a single week at Bath, he had played Macbeth, Benedick, Belville, Bayes and Don John.[31] Nearly a century later, in 1865, the Norwich company was playing *Octoroon* on Monday, Tuesday and Saturday, *Alice Gray* on Wednesday, *Belphegor* on Thursday, and *The Rivals* on Friday, and appearing in a pantomime after the play on all six nights of the week.

3.

"No tricks with a gentleman's wardrobe."

An actor's wardrobe (cant phrase for the things that go in the wardrobe) has always been an object of anxiety and veneration—and, indeed, still is.

4.

"Mr. Lenville presents his kind regards to Mr. Johnson, and will feel obliged if he will inform him at what hour tomorrow morning it will be most convenient to him to meet Mr. L. at the theatre, for the purpose of having his nose pulled in the presence of the company."

Theatrical memoirs are full of stories of jealousies and strife among fellow artists—though more often between the actresses than between the actors. Tate Wilkinson recalls a Mrs. Smith, who was so anxious to prevent the advancement of Mrs. Jordan in her cast of characters that she insisted on claiming her rights within eleven days of her confinement. Mrs. Ward and Mrs. Robinson were equally engaged in deadly struggles with Mrs. Jordan.

5.

"Mrs. Crummles, who was seated [in the green-room] in full regal costume."

No doubt because the dressing-rooms were poky and crowded, artists commonly passed their waiting time in the green-room, a place governed by strict rules of ceremony. Particular seats were considered the property of the leading players. See also page 172f, "Green-room."

6.

"Tights."

Miss Snevellicci was evidently playing a breeches part that night. With Mrs. Crummles arrayed as a queen, the piece could hardly have been a comedy, and the male impersonator would have been out of place in a tragedy.

Doubtless the play was one of those dramas in which the heroine disguises herself as a man—a situation, indeed, in the play in which Nicholas had first beheld her.

Chapter Thirty

1.

"Let me see. This is Wednesday night."

Mr. Lenville's challenge was dated Tuesday night. It was therefore on Wednesday night that Nicholas informed Mrs. Crummles of his impending departure. He then went home as soon as he could. He must have remembered that he had not spoken to Mr. Crummles and returned to the theatre later, for, in the following chapter, Mr. Crummles begins by saying, "This is Wednesday night." The four nights in the week, on which the Crummles company were now playing, were evidently Wednesday, Thursday, Friday, and Saturday.

2.

"We can have positively your last appearance, on Thursday—re-engagement for one night more, on Friday—and, yielding to the wishes of numerous influential patrons who were disappointed in obtaining seats, on Saturday."

Mr. Crummles's famous dogma is plainly confirmed by Charles Rice in a note on the last appearance at Drury Lane, for that season, of Mlle. Duvernay (January 28, 1837). "Mr. Cooper informed the audience that, in consequence of the inability of several parties to gain admission, Mademoiselle Duvernay would perform two more nights. This is as I expected, for managerial falsities are of such common occurrence."[32]

3.

"A brilliant display of fireworks."

Not long before the publication of *Nickleby* the Drury Lane bills were proclaiming a magic flight from the stage to the gallery and back, which a Mr. Blackmore was to accomplish "In the midst of a Splendid Irradiation of Fireworks."

It is small wonder that Georgian theatres were so frequently burned down. At the Norwich theatre they used to obtain spectacular effects by deliberately setting fire to the scenery. As the old homestead disappeared in a blaze, the curtain came down and the stage hands rushed on with buckets of water.[33]

4.

"Ring up Mrs. G., and let the favourite wake 'em."

An early example of that partly playful, partly confident, boast, still familiar in the mouths of comedians.

5.

"Some of those who were not on in the first scene, hurried to the wings, and there stretched their necks to have a peep at him; others stole up into the two little private boxes over the stage-doors, and from that position reconnoitred the London manager."

Actors seem to have been curiously indifferent about showing themselves in the wings in the Georgian theatre. Wilkinson describes Mrs. Jordan at Leeds advancing "as far on the stage, that at the fist-hold of her sister's arm, she was at the very edge of the wing on the stage part."[34] That was in 1785, and, twenty-five years later,

Mrs. Siddons thought nothing of showing herself in the wings while acting with the young Macready.[35] It was, in fact, impossible to avoid being seen from some seats. Most pictures of the Georgian theatre show that the wings were set (because of the grooves) exactly parallel to the footlights—which means that the box seats near the stage must always have had a clear view behind the scenes.

The two little boxes over the stage-doors were originally used both by the audience, and by the actors as part of the scenery. In the early Georgian theatre, whenever actors needed "to find out secrets or plot an escape from a balcony," writes Wilkinson, "they always bowed and thrust themselves into the boxes over the stage-door amidst the company, who were greatly disturbed and obliged to give up their seats."[36] In the later Georgian theatre, when the audience had been banished from the stage, the boxes over the stage-doors remained as part of the permanent scenery. They are shown in the Cruikshank picture opposite page 160, and the Lami picture opposite page 48. See also page 13.

6.
"He went through his part in the two last pieces."

The Portsmouth company gave traditional value for money. Evidently there were at least three plays, a programme comparing with an Ipswich bill for January 3, 1835 (a date exactly in the Crummles period). The Ipswich entertainment consisted in the "last New Popular Comedy", *Married Life*, a song "O give me but my Arab Steed", *Bombastes Furioso*, a duet (by particular desire) "Tell me where is Fancy Bred", and "the truly Laughable Farce", *'Twou'd Puzzle a Conjurer*.

The first relaxation from the long bills of the Georgian theatre seems to have been brought about by accident. Planché records that in 1831 the illness of Miss Foote caused the sudden cancellation of a two-act drama, one of four pieces in the bill at the Olympic. Finding that the audience liked getting out at eleven instead of twelve, Madame Vestris decided on keeping the shorter bill—though it was long enough even then.[37] Five years later, in August, 1836, Charles Rice twice recorded a performance at the Haymarket theatre which lingered on till half-past one, and many years were to pass before a shorter entertainment was generally established.[38] At Norwich in 1865, a ten-scene pantomime was preceded by *The Rivals*, and in 1870 Planché could write in his autobiography that long bills were "still too frequently the practice at more than one theatre." The two-piece bill, a play and a curtain-raiser, survived well into the twentieth century.

7.

"Having been received with unbounded favour and unprecedented applause—so said the bills for next day, which had been printed an hour or two before."

It is particularly interesting to find Dickens scoring this small point. One would hardly hope to find evidence on the practice of early nineteenth-century bill-sticking —but it so happens that a sentence in Elliston's biography contains the exact information required. "In minor theatres, the bills of the following day are printed before the performances of the immediate night are concluded."[39]

REFERENCES

1. The origin and development of the Jolly Jack Tar is discussed at length in the author's *Burlesque Tradition in the English Theatre after 1660* (1952).

2. Mathews, *op. cit.*, vol. 1, p. 67.

3. The little that is known of Mrs. Baker has been assembled by Norma Hodgson in "Sarah Baker (1736/7-1816) 'Governess-General of the Kentish Drama' ", an essay in *Studies in English Theatre History*, printed for The Society for Theatre Research, 1952.

4. *The Georgian Playhouse*, 1948, by Richard Southern contains a photograph of an original piece of this apparatus (discovered at the Theatre Royal, Bristol); and contemporary plans showing the position which the grooves occupied. Mr. Southern writes at length about the English groove system in *The Oxford Companion to the Theatre*, 1951, under "English Playhouse", pp. 238-42.

5. Wilkinson *Memoirs*, 1790, vol. 4, p. 92.

6. Irving, *op. cit.*, p. 69.

7. Wilkinson, *The Wandering Patentee*, vol. 2, p. 103.

8. *Ibid.*, vol. 4, pp. 159-60.

9. See M. Willson Disher, *Blood and Thunder*, 1949, pp. 237-41.

10. Rosenfeld, *op. cit.*, pp. 84, 87.

11. See pp. 43, 81, 128.

12. Wilkinson, *The Wandering Patentee*, vol. 2, pp. 37, 72.

13. Pierce Egan, *The Life of an Actor,* 1904 edition, p. 217.

14. Ryley, *op. cit.*, vol. 3, p. 305.

15. Ryley, *op. cit.*, vol. 4, p. 124.

16. Snagg, *op. cit.*, p. 99.

17. *Memoirs of Thomas Holcroft*, ed. William Hazlitt, 1816, vol. 2, pp. 55-6.

18. See p. 148.

19. *The Private Correspondence of David Garrick*, vol. 1, p. 46.

20. This bill is quoted by Tate Wilkinson in *The Wandering Patentee*, vol. 2, p. 203. The earliest English play-bill still existing—of 1672—is preserved in the Public Record Office, London. See an article by George Speaight in *Theatre Notebook*, vol. 6, No. 2, 1952.

21. Davies, *Garrick*, vol. 1, p. 159.

22. T. L. G. Burley, *Playhouses and Players of East Anglia*, 1928, p. 6.

23. Wilkinson, *Memoirs*, vol. 4, pp. 68-9.

24. Wilkinson, *The Wandering Patentee*, vol. 3, p. 171.

25. See p. 107.

26. Snagg, *op. cit.*, p. 59.

27. See p. 47*f.*

28. *The Private Correspondence of David Garrick*, vol. 1, p. 32.

29. Dunlap, *op. cit.*, vol. 2, p. 291.

30. *The Dickensian*, Spring, 1949.

31. *The Private Correspondence of David Garrick*, vol. 2, p. 16.

32. Rice, *op. cit.*, p. 18.

33. Bosworth Harcourt, *Theatre Royal, Norwich*, 1903, p. 3.

34. Wilkinson, *The Wandering Patentee*, vol. 2, p. 262.

35. See p. 42.

36. Wilkinson, *Memoirs*, vol. 4, p. 112.

37. Planché, *op. cit.*, pp. 128-9.

38. Rice, *op. cit.*, pp. 2, 4.

39. Raymond, *op. cit.*, p. 411.

VII

CUSTOM AND BEHAVIOUR
IN THE GEORGIAN THEATRE

"When found make a note of."
Captain Cuttle: *Dombey and Son*

VII

THESE notes are not intended as a comprehensive catalogue of dramatic phraseology. They are a magpie collection of theatrical curiosities, not a dictionary of the playhouse, and they deal more with people than with things. Technical terms, most of which have been fully defined in *The Oxford Companion to the Theatre* (1951), are not included. Indeed, it is an indication of the mass of our theatrical inheritance that this list overlaps hardly at all with that indispensable work.

In three entries in this chapter—"Breeches Part", "Clap-trap", "Star"—I have been able to point to earlier uses of the words than those quoted by Sir St. Vincent Troubridge when he corrected the *Oxford English Dictionary* in *Notes and Queries* (1941–2). "Clap-trap" (1741)—Troubridge confined himself to the word inverted, "trap clap" (1827)—and "Star" (1740) are clear cases. For "Breeches Part" (Troubridge 1779) the evidence is indirect: the word is quoted by Tate Wilkinson (1790) in the record of a conversation of 1759.

Earlier in this book direct or indirect evidence may be found of four other words or phrases in records earlier than those noted by Troubridge. "The first music," is indicated by Wilkinson (1795) in quoting a play-bill of 1734, and Thomas Davies in his *Memoirs of the Life of David Garrick* (1780) uses the exact phrase, "the second music". (See page 121.) "The Last Musick" is mentioned in *The World in the Moon* by Elkanah Settle (1697), which is 83 years earlier than the date (1780) given in *Notes and Queries*. Indirect evidence of "dress rehearsal" (Troubridge, 1828) is to be found in Munden's biography. Published as late as 1844, it contains a reference to dress rehearsals in 1790. Not clear evidence of the words, it is at least good evidence of the fact. (See page 34.)

I have also been able to give in this chapter an early date for one stage phrase not mentioned in the *Oxford English Dictionary* or by Troubridge: "Between the Scenes" (1737), obsolete variation of the normal "Behind the Scenes."

APOLOGIES

The readiness of the Georgian audience to respond to the stage was the best ingredient in its character. The worst ingredient was its vicious lust for authority. In the eighteenth and early nineteenth centuries there was one grade of society conveniently below everyone: the actors were the bottom, the acknowledged servants of the public, and every member of that public, however lowly, claimed a natural right to command them. The Georgian audience could be generous when it was well pleased, but there was never a time when it was disposed to accept the least disappointment or to abide the smallest opposition to its wishes; and on any provocation it took an indecent delight in exacting apologies from the players.

Sometimes apologies were justly due, as when that redoubtable virago, Mrs. Montague, spoilt a performance of *The Rivals* at York by refusing to appear in the last scene; but far more often the audience were not even in the right, and insisted on apologies merely for the

9. Contending for a seat. *From a coloured engraving by Theodore Lane.*

pleasure of demonstrating their authority. Kemble was called on to apologize because he had requested a lady to stop talking; Murray, because he had had a quarrel with a local nob in a Wakefield bar-room; Moody, because he prevented a rioter from setting fire to Drury Lane. None of the three did apologize, for they were conscious of no fault; but where an audience was united and a player in any degree guilty, an apology was always exacted, even from actors as eminent as Cooke or Kean; and if the offence were large and the actor of no great consequence, he was often forced to ask for pardon on his knees.

A remark in *The Times* of December 28, 1818, shows how seriously this claim of authority could be regarded by a responsible person. The Drury Lane pantomime had not been a success, the curtain had dropped in a tumult of disapproval, and Bradbury the clown, who came forward to announce the piece for repetition, had been refused a hearing. "By-the-by", wrote the critic of *The Times* after describing the scene, "we may mention that this Clown, before he is again allowed to exhibit his anticks, should be required to make an apology to the public for his persevering resistance to their will, and the impertinent manner in which he testified his dissatisfaction at their decision."

So thought the second night's audience (though the noisier part of it was not likely to have had any knowledge of *The Times* criticism) and before the piece was allowed to proceed Bradbury was duly forced to beg forgiveness.

The desire of the audience to assert their authority seems to have been much stronger than their desire to enjoy the entertainment. If the patrons of the drama were

K

determined to exact an apology, they stopped the play the moment the offending actor appeared on the scene, and for all they cared the play might be interrupted by minutes of shouting and speech making, or even not finished at all.

BEHIND THE SCENES

"If your Delight lies behind the Scenes, you'll have enough on't to Night; for, after the Play's done, I hear the Actors have a general Practice of the Musick and Machines of some part of their New Opera."
The World in the Moon, by Elkanah Settle, 1697.

"Behind the scenes" is a phrase which belongs to the common coin of conversation, and few who use it would think that it meant anything more than being, in a general sort of way, on the actors' side of the curtain. In the Georgian theatre the scenery consisted, principally, of flats at the back (which drew together or drew apart in two halves) and wings which slid on and off. These pieces of scenery were known as "the scenes", and to be behind them was literally to be standing in such a position that you were obscured from the audience, or presumed to be obscured, by the scene. Actors or visitors watching the play from the wings were "behind the scenes"—and that the words implied a particular location seems indicated by a speech in Colley Cibber's *Love Makes a Man* (1700): "I do know London pretty well, and the Side-box, sir, and behind the Scenes; ay, and the Green-Room, and all the Girls and Women-Actresses there."[1]

Another phrase, which has not survived but which is even plainer, was "between the scenes", meaning the space between one wing and the next. "Sir," says the Author in Fielding's *Eurydice* (1737), "if you please to sit down with me between the scenes, I shall be glad of your opinion of my piece." Boswell adds one valuable word. On the occasion when Johnson threw a man into the pit at Lichfield for stealing his seat, he had been sitting "between the side scenes".

At the beginning of his tenancy of Drury Lane Garrick had announced that he could not admit the public to the stage during the performance, but he did not absolutely get rid of visitors until the enlargement of Drury Lane in 1763, and at other houses even after that date they were still sometimes accommodated with seats "between the scenes", or "behind the scenes". "A new opera by Bach was so crowded that there were ladies standing behind the scenes during the whole performance," wrote Horace Walpole to Lord Hertford, on January 27, 1765. The year before, when the Prince of Brunswick was at the opera, ladies had sat "between the scenes", and so great was the crush in the body of the theatre that the box doors had been opened to allow a glimpse of the house to the people who crowded the corridor and even sat on the stairs—clear proof that place and fashion weighed much heavier with the Georgian aristocracy than any genuine regard for the art of the theatre.

At Covent Garden the warning that no person would be admitted behind the scenes was continued in the advertisements for many years, but it is clear that privileged persons on special occasions did manage to find accommodation on the stage up to the very end of the Georgian period. When Queen Victoria visited Covent

Garden in 1838, Macready received numerous applications for admission behind the scenes, "which I was obliged to answer as I could."[2] And in 1840, when the Queen and Prince Albert, then newly married, visited Covent Garden, "my wife is mad to see the sight at Covent Garden on Friday," wrote Thackeray to J. R. Planché; "can you get me a ticket to go behind the scenes?" The letter was accompanied by a comic picture of the royal pair in their box, and Charles Mathews promised Thackeray seats on condition that he gave him a similar drawing. And so, writes Planché, "Mr. and Mrs. Thackeray were amongst the closely packed throng of privileged persons who enjoyed the wonderful sight the house presented, viewed from the stage, as the curtain rose to the first bars of the National Anthem on that memorable evening."[3]

The report in *The Times* of February 29 shows that these privileged persons were at first actually on the stage in full view of the audience, for the rise of the curtain disclosed "besides the singers, a party of visitors, perhaps more numerous than there generally are on such occasions. . . . Immediately after the conclusion of the anthem the persons on the stage receded to the right and left, and the last scene of *The Fortunate Isles* was discovered."

At benefit performances in the early Georgian theatre not only were the wings crowded, but extra seats were built up at the back of the stage so that one audience faced another. "An audience behind the curtain up to the clouds," wrote Tate Wilkinson, with Romeo "breaking open the supposed tomb, which was no more than a screen on those nights set up, and Mrs. Cibber prostrating herself on an old couch, covered with black cloth, as the tomb of the Capulets, with at least (on a great benefit night) two hundred persons behind her."[4] This grotesque device for accommodating more people was discontinued in the later, and larger, Georgian theatre, but it was not so absolutely forgotten that Elliston could not revive it for a monster benefit performance held at the Opera House in 1804.

In the early theatre a place behind the scenes was a plain opportunity for the malicious. Thomas Davies has a pleasant story of a strolling company playing *Cato* at Windsor in 1713. "What do I hear?" cried the atrocious performer of Juba. "My Lord Malpas," says Davies, "wilfully mistaking the actor, loudly said, from behind the scenes, *Upon my word, sir, I do not know: I think you had better be anywhere else*: and this joke, I believe, put an end to the play."[5]

Few people find their way behind the scenes nowadays, but there will never be an absolute end to the admission there of privileged persons. Gladstone was a frequent visitor on the stage of the Lyceum. Irving kept a special seat for him, protected from draught by a velvet curtain, with a stage hand standing by to guard the prime minister from being hit on the head by the roller curtain.

A modern reference can be found in Augustus John's *Chiaroscuro* (1952). "We attended a performance of *Tess* at Dorchester: Hardy, hearing that I was present, sent word to invite me to meet him 'behind': I was thus able to watch the play from the wings."[6]

BENEFIT

At the present day professional cricketers and footballers have benefits. So do performers in seaside pierrot troupes. Benefits in the theatre died when the old provincial stock companies gave place to the touring companies, and when the large London company, engaged for a season, gave place to the small company, engaged for the duration of a run.

In the Georgian theatre an actor's benefit performance was more important than his salary, and a clear agreement on the matter was included in the terms of his contract. The actor had the use of the theatre for the night. He drew up an attractive bill, persuaded as many important actors as possible to appear for him, and himself disposed of tickets for the performance. Wealthy patrons often gave an actor a monetary present on the occasion of his benefit, and between gifts and tickets a prominent actor in a London theatre sometimes cleared several hundred pounds. Cooke's benefit at Covent Garden in 1801 amounted to £500.[7]

The property bill had to be reckoned against the receipts. Nor could the management be expected to grant the actor an entirely free use of the house. Expenses for lights and staff had to be met, not counting the loss to the management of the night's business. A fixed charge was made for the use of the theatre, and that sum had to be deducted from the actor's takings.

At Lincoln's Inn Fields in 1724 the house charge was £40. A few years later some actors were being charged £50, others £60. At Covent Garden in the '40's, the charge varied, according to the terms of the actor's contract, between £40 and £60, and for many years not much more than £60 was the normal charge at both the great houses. Towards the end of the century the charge mounted steeply. At Covent Garden in 1800 it was raised from £140 to £160, and was a principal cause of complaint in the quarrel of that year between the actors and the proprietors.[8]

Benefit money was collected in two ways—by tickets sold in advance by the actor, and by money taken at the door. The custom of the proprietors was to hold fast to the money taken at the door as part payment for the house charge. The difference between the door takings and the charge is recorded in the accounts as Mr. Laluze's, or Mrs. Horton's, or Mr. Roberts's "deficiency", and is duly settled by the actor on the next day or soon after. Early in the century it may be questioned if the management always received the full sum. In the Lincoln's Inn Fields accounts an entry frequently notes that the management has kept the door money, £23 6s. 6d. or £16 6s. 6d. but that Mr. Salle or Mr. Berriman or Mr. Rochetti has been allowed to give a note for the remainder of the charge. Plainly the management were at a disadvantage. They could freeze on to the money paid at the door, but the price of tickets sold privately by the actor had already gone into his pocket.[9]

If an actor were sufficiently important he might make particular stipulations, even for a benefit free of all expenses. Cooke had made no such agreement at Covent Garden in 1801, but the managers were so delighted with the success of the new actor that they made him a present of a clear benefit.

In the country an important visitor could make a lot of money. Munden's benefit at Liverpool in 1804 earned £278. Moreover the star could command a benefit in every centre that he visited. The benefits of ordinary performers in small provincial theatres were arranged on less liberal principles. At Norwich, in the middle of the eighteenth century, the house charge was £21. But a large house charge was an anxiety to both player and management, and later benefits were usually arranged on a sharing basis. In Tate Wilkinson's company the actors had yearly benefits at Hull, Leeds, and York, with an equal division of the takings between manager and actor above £4. A few years later, in the early nineteenth century, benefits on the Norwich circuit were shared with the manager after the first £10. A visitor, not of the first fame, but a cut above the resident company, could sometimes stipulate for a guaranteed minimum. Mrs. Esten's benefit, for instance, in August 1790, at York, was "secured" at £60. This benefit proved a humiliating failure, and if Mrs. Esten had not been secured she would not have received very much. It did sometimes happen that a benefit resulted in a positive loss. Mrs. Jordan is said to have suffered such a disaster at the outset of her career, in Ireland. The legend goes that a party of young admirers made such a row in the theatre that they forced the manager to give her another—this time free of charges. Everard has several records of unsuccessful benefits, including a pathetic story of an Italian dancer who thought a benefit was one of the necessary and unavoidable expenses of the English stage.

A benefit was a serious anxiety to the performer; he was obliged to canvass, to leave bills from door to door, to wait upon influential patrons. Some of the better managements banned these degrading applications, but that canvassing lingered up to the end of the Georgian period is proved by the story of Miss Snevellicci's great bespeak, when, after many calls, that favourite actress "pledged herself to a bill of fare which was comprehensive enough, if it had no other merit . . . and they returned home, pretty well exhausted with the business of the day."

A form of benefit which brought in very little but had no risks or house charges attached to it was the custom of "taking tickets". By this arrangement an actor was allowed to sell as many tickets as he could, and to keep one half of the proceeds. The other half went to the management.

By the end of the Georgian period benefit conditions in London were as severely limited as they were in the provinces. An account book of Macready's management at Drury Lane (now in the Enthoven collection) shows that actors usually shared equally with the management above a certain figure. Miss Horton's benefit account (May 7, 1842) is marked "share after £40." Mr. H. Phillips had the same terms on May 12. On May 23 Mr. Anderson shared over £50. The reward was not great. Miss Horton netted £47 17s. 8d., Phillips £53 3s. 6d.

It is impossible to track down all the different dates at which the custom of the benefit finally expired in different places. Irving took his last Lyceum benefit in 1887 and Ellen Terry hers in 1895. A curiously late example is the benefit which was taken on the last night of the Exeter pantomime by Percy Dunsford (d. 1940), manager of the Theatre Royal. These used to be announced as "Mr. Percy Dunsford's Benefit and Great Fun Night", and the manager always appeared in one of the leading parts. The last advertisement in the Exeter *Express and Echo* (February 3) is for the performance on Saturday, February 4, 1928. In the following year the "Great Fun Night" is billed but there is no mention of a benefit. In February 1930 there was no "Great Fun Night" but Mr. Dunsford did act "as the schoolmaster in the place of Mr. Crowe, causing much amusement." (*Devon and Exeter Gazette*, February 10.)

The author's payment was also made by benefit performance, less the house charge, which in Garrick's time was (for authors) at first sixty guineas, and after the enlargement of Drury Lane, seventy guineas.[10] In 1775 Charles Dibdin agreed to pay eighty guineas. An author could make a fair sum of money on this system. In 1768 three nights of *Zenobia* brought Arthur Murphy £467 6s. 6d.; in 1775 three nights of *Matilda* (the 3rd, 8th, and 9th) brought Francklin £336 7s.—in each case after deduction of house charges. But it was not a fair system, for the author's nights might coincide with poor houses even though the play were a success. When Holcroft's *Duplicity* was played at Covent Garden for the author's benefit, in 1781, it did not clear the expenses of the house. In 1784 Holcroft wrote to the Drury Lane management suggesting a salary instead of author's nights. Nothing came of this.

It was Frederic Reynolds who made the first successful moves towards a fairer system. By agreement with Harris, for the comedy *Notoriety*, in 1791, after deducting £100 for expenses, he was to receive the profits of the third, sixth, ninth, and twentieth nights. This arrangement brought him £420—a decent reward, though the risk of receiving nothing still remained. In 1793 a similar agreement for *How to Grow Rich* brought him, including the sale of the copyright, £620. When his fourth comedy, *The Rage*, was produced in 1794, Reynolds proposed a new system. "Fearing that a *benefit*, at Covent Garden, might prove a *loss*, and that I was more likely to receive a *call*[11] for my jokes, than a *dividend*, I proposed to Mr. Harris to make a new arrangement." £33 6s. 8d. was to be paid on each of the first nine nights, and £100 on the twentieth. This plan brought him less (£400—£500, with the sale of the copyright), but the money was certain, provided the play was successful. He was paid on the same system at Drury Lane in 1797. In 1799 yet another agreement was made with Harris by which Reynolds was paid £100 on the third, sixth, and ninth nights, £50 on the fifteenth and twentieth nights and £150 for the copyright—which secured his possible profits at £550. In 1808 he received £600, which indicates some further agreement for £50.

According to Reynolds both Morton and Mrs. Inchbald sold their plays before production, and received considerably higher fees than he did. No arrangement seems to have been made at this time to reward the continued success of a piece after the twentieth performance. Royalties on a percentage basis for the whole run of a play were not established till 1860.

BESPEAK

The bespeak performance was a Georgian device for getting a good house. In imitation of the royal command, the local big-wig was easily persuaded to request the performance of a particular play on a night when he would be pleased to patronize the theatre. The custom was flattering to the patron because it acknowledged his importance. It suited the theatre manager because it ensured the sale of many box seats (at more than the normal price if the big-wig were anything of a gentleman)

and because the fashionable occasion was certain to
attract a good audience in other parts of the house.

In the absence of a bespeak, managements were very
fond of announcing vaguely that a play was being performed at the particular desire of persons unspecified.
Henry Fielding's "Juvenal's Sixth Satire Modernised in
Burlesque Verse" has the following footnote to the line,

> Nor play-bills By Desire, are put up.

"A constant puff at the head of our play-bills; designed
to allure people to the house, who go thither more for
the sake of the company than of the play; but which has
proved so often fallacious (*plays having been acted at the
particular desire of several ladies of quality, when there hath
not been a single lady of quality in the house*) that at present
it hath very little signification."

About a hundred years later Mr. Vincent Crummles was
still practising these managerial arts. See also page 124.

BETWEEN THE SCENES

See "Behind the Scenes."

BONES

One of the actor's privileges in the London Georgian
playhouse was the right to certain bone tickets which
admitted the holder free of charge. Engraved with the
name of the actor to whom they belonged, these bones
were loaned by him to his friends for individual performances, and returned to him, or to the box office.
"Please to give Mr. Sourby Mrs. Davenport's Box
Bones. A. H. Davenport. 1st Sept. 1810," runs a note

preserved in the Enthoven Collection. Another: "Dear Charles I have recᵈ. Two Box Bones—can you spare two more W. Blanchard."

The Enthoven Collection contains a valuable memorandum dated November 18, 1816, signed by E. Warren, inspector of checks, which gives an indication of what the performers' privileges were at Drury Lane, and shows that the actors' claim to free seats was fourfold. There were orders, bones, privileged tickets, and the free list; and the four things were not the same.

Performers' Privileges

Those Performers whose Salaries amount to £12 & upwards are entitled to send in (when Bones are permitted) *two Double Tickets* to the *Boxes*, & the Same to the Gallery. When Bones are stopped—*One* Double ticket to each Place.

Those Performers whose Salaries amount to £5 & upward are entitled to two Bones to the Boxes.
[Two words obscure]

The Bones are stopped when the Manager thinks proper.

Those Performers whose Salaries amount to £3 & upwards, are entitled to the Free List.

The Privilege of sending in One Double ticket to the Boxes & the same to the Gallery is *never* taken away.

No clear sense can be made of this until it is realized that the bone and the ticket were different things. They both ended in a free seat, but they were not the same. The rules may be restated as follows:

1. All players with salaries of £12 could always demand 2 seats in the boxes and 2 in the gallery.

2. The bone tickets also obtained seats—but only on nights when it suited the management to allow them. When bone tickets were allowed, actors with high salaries were also allowed double the number of ordinary tickets.

3. Actors with salaries above £3 were on the Free List—which meant that they had a right to a seat for themselves when not playing.

4. Orders—which are not mentioned in this memorandum—were outside ordinary rights and privileges. They are discussed later under their own heading.

Drury Lane tally sheets, preserved in the Enthoven Collection, confirm the terms of this memorandum, and reveal a traffic in free seats quite sufficient to explain the eternal bankruptcy of the Georgian playhouse. Written down the right hand margin of each night's tally is the number of orders, followed by a list of the tickets claimed by each actor, the number of bones, and the number of press tickets. On January 2, 1816, for instance, box orders were 267, pit orders 40, gallery orders 22; bones were 69; actors' tickets were 84 in the boxes, 56 in the gallery; and the newspaper seats in boxes and pit amounted to 90. Free privilege passes were 19, making 647 non-paying seats, not counting the subscription seats, unproductive in the same way as certain seats at the Albert Hall are unproductive. 19 was low for the free list: on November 9 the number was 101. The newspapers had free seats in huge numbers at *every* performance. On November 25, 1817, a new heading "Cards" appears on the tally—but "Newspapers" is absent on that day and the two words never subsequently appear together. One heading "N. Cards" seems to make it clear that "Cards" and "Newspapers" are the same entry. Newspaper men have always been addicted to whipping out a card.

A tally sheet for December 13, 1816, is reproduced opposite page 208.

The entry "Bones" is often absent from the list, but there does not seem to have been a close restriction on the number of tickets given to actors. The tally for February 5, 1817, notes that Mr. Rae has had "one Double ticket too much"; but actors are often credited with more than their due number: on January 17, 1817, 40 tickets are recorded against Kean's name. The author of the farce, *Frightened to Death*, seems to have entertained his entire acquaintance. In various parts of the house, on different nights, he was allotted as many as 86, 62, 68, 143, and 157 free seats.

It is plain that there was a gradation in the value of these privileges. A ticket was a ticket, nothing less. If you had a ticket you were in. A bone was something which would always be honoured—but it was not on every night that they could be used. An order was a request—frequently granted but not positively guaranteed.

In the Drury Lane tally sheets in the Enthoven Collection (1803–9 and 1816–19) the word 'bone' disappears after the end of the 1816-17 season.

In the Dublin Theatre a similar privilege was acknowledged in silver. "Two free silver tickets for the admission of my friends" were given to Thomas Snagg in 1773.[12]

See also "Orders", page 188*f*.

BREECHES PARTS

"Ask Mr. Barry what he thinks my daughter came over to Ireland for?—Then if you do not know, I will tell you Sir—the breeches parts Sir! and she expects *all* the breeches parts Sir—and now you know Bet's mind." So Mrs. White, attacking Mr. Younger in Dublin on behalf of her daughter, Bet, in December 1759.[13]

Breeches parts was the accepted name for those dashing juvenile male leads in which the ladies of the Georgian and the Victorian theatres delighted to display themselves. Most of the great comedy actresses were of the same mind as Bet White. They fancied themselves in breeches and appeared not only as straight heroes (Lionel in *Lionel and Clarissa*) and jolly blades (Sir Harry in *The Constant Couple*) but also in strong parts (Macheath in *The Beggar's Opera*) tragedy parts (Hamlet, Romeo, Ion[14]) and sometimes in low comedy (Scrub in *The Beaux' Stratagem*). A Brighton play-bill of 1870 announced Miss Fanny Harrison in the muscular hero part of Tom Tug in *The Waterman*.

In the provinces the breeches tradition was often up-held by a shortage of men in the companies. Between 1723 and 1765 as many as twenty-seven Shakespearean male parts were played by women in the Kent circuit alone.[15] A woman might make a good thing of Osric, but Cornwall and Albany in *King Lear* can only have been given to women from reasons of acute necessity.

There were those who disapproved of the male impersonator, including some actresses who sternly refused to risk their reputations by wearing breeches. But in spite of criticism breeches parts remained popular throughout the whole eighteenth century and in the

11. Spectators between the scenes at Grimaldi's farewell benefit. *From an etching by George Cruikshank.*

12. Breeches Part: Louisa Nesbitt in *The Young King* at the Haymarket Theatre, 1837. *From a coloured lithograph by J. Deffett Francis.*

nineteenth century became an essential characteristic of Victorian extravaganza. Even in the twentieth century the tradition has not died easily. In the wartime season of 1915 Sybil Thorndike played Prince Hal, Lear's Fool, and Ferdinand at the Old Vic; and earlier, on tour with Ben Greet, she had played Launcelot Gobbo. Marie Löhr has played L'Aiglon, and Yvonne Printemps, Mozart; and in the 1920's Mrs. Acton Bond was touring *Hamlet* with an all woman cast. The male impersonator has slipped out of the theatre of today; she does not even make many appearances on the vaudeville stage; but the tradition of the breeches part still remains, enshrined in the figures of Peter Pan and the Principal Boy. See also "Traditions of the Pantomime", pages 218*f*.

BURLETTA

Kitty Clive defined "that new thing, a burletto" in *The Rehearsal; or Bays in Petticoats* (1750) as "a kind of poor Relation to an Opera"—which was well judged. A burletta was something less than a comic opera: it was operatic farce, and never a full length entertainment.

Mrs. Clive was alluding to the Italian artists at the Haymarket theatre. Earlier references occur in two letters of Horace Walpole's. December 2, 1748: "The burlettas are begun; I think, not decisively liked or condemned yet: their success is certainly not rapid. . . ." And, March 23, 1749, "The burlettas don't much succeed, though there never were two better comedians than Perceti and Laschi."

Italian burlettas were introduced at Covent Garden in the season 1753–4, and were continued in the following two seasons. Their success was small, according to Tate

L

Wilkinson, but Horace Walpole said the people were "transported with them." Certainly the success was sufficient to inspire native imitations.

The earliest examples of the burletta in English were, naturally, "taken from the Italian", such as *The Tutor* (1759) and *The Stratagem* (1761). But in 1762 (Dublin) Kane O'Hara's *Midas* (Covent Garden 1764) set a model for the English burletta which was never superseded. No other burletta was ever so successful except one adapted by the same author from Fielding's burlesque, *Tom Thumb* (1780). In the strife between the two Dublin theatres the original *Midas*, at Capel Street, was produced not so much in imitation of, as in opposition to, the Italian burlettas which were having a great success at Smock Alley.

The later growth and popularity of the burletta was intimately connected with the policies of the minor theatres. The Licensing Act of 1737 had confined the "legitimate drama" to Drury Lane and Covent Garden, and allowed only limited licences for music and dancing to the smaller houses. In the burlettas the managers of the minor theatres perceived an opportunity for evading the full intentions of the law. Almost anything could be turned into a burletta, so long as the dialogue was sung not spoken. Macready reports that he saw Elliston in 1809 at the Surrey theatre, acting *Macbeth* as a pantomime, and Captain Macheath in *The Beggar's Opera*, with Gay's dialogue "thrown into jingling rhyme".[16] Another classic converted by Elliston into a burletta was *The Beaux' Stratagem*. Adaptations like these were made by the dozen for particular theatres. Only rarely were such versions printed, and not often, indeed, were they repeated.

In 1830 Colman defined the burletta in *Random Records* as "*a drama in rhyme,* and which is *entirely musical*; a short comick piece, consisting of *recitative* and *singing,* wholly accompanied, more or less, by the orchestra."[17] Wholly accompanied, more or less: the muddled phrase is significant: performers were not always careful to vocalize the recitative part. Many violations of the law passed unnoticed, and many others were undoubtedly winked at. Eventually, "after much controversy both in and out of court," writes Planché, "we were desired to understand [as burlettas] dramas containing not less than five pieces of vocal music in each act, and which were also, with one or two exceptions, not to be found in the *repertoire* of the patent houses."[18]

A minor theatre might legally produce a burletta, and the managers clung eagerly to the description so long as they had need of it. The emancipation of the minor theatres by the new legislation of 1843 removed the need, and the burlettas disappeared immediately, but not without exercising a powerful influence upon the extravaganzas which followed them. Both forms were largely concerned with farcical kings and queens, gods and goddesses, and were a mixture of songs and rhymed couplets. The main difference lay in the fact that the couplets of the extravaganza were spoken; and, because they were spoken, it became necessary to bring a larger wit to the business of writing them.

The word burletta lingered longer in the provinces than in London. A Leeds programme for September 10, 1866, advertises *Macbeth,* followed by a song, a Grand Pas Espagnole, and then "the ever-popular Burletta (by Stirling Coyne Esq.) entitled *The Water Witches*".

CAST

In the twentieth century the word cast is used only to indicate the list of persons interpreting the characters in a play. In the Georgian theatre it indicated, equally, the list of characters that an actor was accustomed to perform. Thus, Tate Wilkinson writes, "Her own written cast"—meaning the list of characters supplied to him by Mrs. Rivers.[19] Again, Tate Wilkinson writes in a letter engaging Knight: "I know your cast perfectly well. You shall play any two parts you like, but it is impossible to ascertain a cast. If Mr. Bennett goes, there will be plenty."[20] Meaning that Wilkinson knew Knight's list of characters, but was uncertain, till the company was fixed, how many of them, beyond two, he would be able to annex. Again, "On his being engaged, Mr. Holcroft was desired by Mr. Sheridan to give in his cast of parts to Mr. Hopkins, the prompter."[21]

It was a practice which had to go. "The right to the possession of his cast of characters, a most important privilege which appertained to the Actor, has of late years been so constantly violated, that it can scarcely be said to exist," wrote the actors in their dispute with the managers in 1800. But the Lord Chamberlain's opinion was clean against them. "As to the right claimed by the Performers of keeping a cast of characters, it appears to me that the Proprietors have a power of employing the Performers in such characters as they think proper."

The word is frequently, and erroneously, spelt 'caste' in modern theatre programmes—a worse fatuity than the companion affectation of 'artiste', because 'caste' has an entirely separate derivation and means something totally different.

CLAP-TRAP

Aaron Hill used the word clap-trap in 1741, which is a long time before it appeared in any dictionary. "You must have remarked," he writes to Mallet, "how much the *claps* in a *Tragedy* can contribute to its *success* on the *Stage*—as well by raising the *spirits* of the *actors*, as by awakening the *hopes* of an *audience*." Unfortunately, he says, most actors "indiscreetly *run on*, when they do not *foresee* such applause, and *lose* it, by not stopping on a *thought*, that invites it, unless the sense is cut short, so as, in a manner, to *constrain* them to allow it the *weight*, that is proper to it." To this end a writer of skill ought "to prepare, in all his *strong*, or his *passionate* speeches, as many *Clap-traps*, for the most part, as *couplets*." Hill wrote several letters about the value of applause—claps he usually calls it—but this is the only one in which 'clap-trap' appears.[22]

There are two kinds of clap-trap: the trap set by the author and the trap set by the performer. Frederick Reynolds (1826)[23] gives a good embracing description of the author's clap-trap, when he refers to Sheridan as having "despised the faults of another school, trap claps. Not a word in the *School for Scandal* is to be found of Laws, Jack Tars, Innocence, an Englishman's *castellum*, or Liberty."

Later writers were not so fastidious. The word is used uncritically, in its technical sense, in the biographies of Fitzball (1859) and Munden (1844). In 1802, we are told, Munden played Peter, a British seaman, in *The Cabinet* by Thomas Dibdin, "and sang some clap-trap songs, adapted to the times, with great applause."[24] And Fitzball describes (in a passage already quoted)[25] how he contrived to pop a clap-trap into the mouth of a character, much to the satisfaction of his manager.

An early example of the actor's, as opposed to the author's, trap for applause may be found in *The Female Wits* (1697) where Marsilia says, "Dear Mrs. *Knight*, in this Speech, stamp as Queen *Statira* does, that always gets a Clap." Many years later Thomas Davies, in his biography of David Garrick (1780), was defining the word more closely—an "anxious exertion at the close of a speech, both in look and behaviour, which is called by the comedians a clap-trap." And Thomas Snagg, writing in 1810 of his theatre days forty years earlier, says, "I was not unacquainted with some of the necessary clap-traps and how to exit with a becoming flourish." Leigh Hunt exactly confirms these descriptions in his *Critical Essays on the Performers of the London Theatres* (1807). The clap-trap, he says, "consists in nothing more, than in gradually raising the voice as the speech draws to a conclusion, making an alarming outcry on the last four or five lines, or suddenly dropping them into a tremulous but energetic undertone, and with a vigorous jerk of the right arm rushing off the stage. All this astonishes the galleries; they are persuaded it must be something very fine, because it is so important and so unintelligible, and they clap for the sake of their own reputation."[26]

The last few words are also a sound comment on the modern tendency in Radio audiences to clap jokes instead of laughing at them. They clap "for the sake of their own reputations"—to make it clearly understood that they have seen the point. All radio and vaudeville comedians are clap-trappers, though there is an aristocracy among them who recognize the supremacy of laughter. "I prefer the laughter to the applause," I have heard Arthur Askey remark to a studio audience.

Except at the curtain call the clap-trap is an art very little practised in the serious theatre today.

DAMNING THE PLAY

Damning the play was so common a practice in the Georgian theatre that the phrase ranks as a cliché. Plays were not judged by subsequent bookings or subsequent criticisms. They were judged in the theatre during the presentation, and when an attempt was made to "give out the play for repetition" at the end, a piece was either approved or damned by the loudly expressed opinions of the audience. Judgment was swayed by many things besides a critical consideration of the merits of the play. A piece might be damned in order to attack the manager, as a rebuff to some unpopular actor, or as the consequence of the smallest affront imagined by that prickly audience. Thus Fielding, in a prologue of 1742 already quoted,[27] remarks that the omission of the prologue would be most unfortunate—

Besides, 'twould be quite unprecedented—and I dare say,
Such an attempt, Sir, would make them damn the play.

Often, a piece was damned before it had even begun, by persons, who, for reasons of spite against the author, were determined that it should not succeed. Theatrical histories contain dozens of stories of organized opposition to a play. Here it may be interesting to quote a story of unsuccessful opposition, a new piece of evidence from the recently published *London Journal* of

James Boswell. On January 19, 1763, Boswell, Dempster and Erskine attended Drury Lane for the first performance of *Elvira* and "as the play would probably be bad, and as Mr. David Malloch, the author, who has changed his name to David Mallet, Esq., was an arrant puppy, we determined to exert ourselves in damning it." Accordingly they established themselves in the pit (prudently addressing each other by assumed names) and with oak cudgels in their hands and shrill sounding cat-calls in their pockets, they waited their opportunity to destroy the presumptuous Mr. Mallet. They hissed the prologue and "did what we could during the first act," but found to their disappointment that the majority of the audience were disposed to let it pass.[28]

Arthur Murphy was less fortunate. In the Advertisement to *Three Weeks after Marriage* he writes: "The following scenes were offered to the Public in January 1764; but a party of that species of CRITICS, whom the love of mischief sometimes assembles at the theatre, being unwilling to hear, the piece was *damned*."

Compare, also, Horace Walpole in a letter of March 11, 1748: "There has been a new comedy, called *The Foundling*; far from good, but it took. Lord Hobart and some more young men made a party to damn it merely for the love of damnation." Writing thirty years later to Mason, March 16, 1778, Walpole declared that nothing would induce him to venture his own tragedy, *The Mysterious Mother*, on the stage, "not from superabundant modesty, but from the abusive spirit of the times. I have no notion of presenting oneself coolly to a savage mob to be torn to pieces."

Strangely enough damning was not always confined to the audience. If the actors did not like a play they were not above taking no pains to make it a success. Charles Lamb said that John Kemble "had the art of diffusing a complacent, equable dullness (which you knew not where to quarrel with) over a piece which he did not like." Other performers were less subtle. There was an actors', and even a manager's, conspiracy against Sarah Gardner's *The Marriage Advertisement* (1777). See also page 31, for the fiasco of Fanny Burney's tragedy in 1795.

Apart from malicious opposition the phrase long remained in the theatre as the normal description for a failure. Macready noted in his diary, April 7, 1838: "The operetta of *Windsor Castle* was in active process of damnation as I left the theatre."

DEAD SHARES

Small touring companies worked on a sharing basis, takings being divided into as many shares as there were players, plus four. The four shares were allotted to the manager in consideration of his scenery, wardrobe, properties, and general organization. The remainder were divided among the players. If the manager were a player, as he usually was, he got another share that way. If his wife or children acted, and they usually did, more shares came to the manager on that account. Holcroft worked with a manager who collected eleven shares out of twenty-four. It was those four shares, which went to the manager anyhow, which were called dead shares.

When Whiteley caught one of his actors pocketing some of the takings at Stamford, he brought the culprit into the green-room saying, "Come, Ladies and Gentlemen—you must have a kick a-piece, and I'll take four for the dead shares."

FREEDOM OF THE HOUSE

Free entry to the theatre was afforded to the authors of all plays, prologues or epilogues, performed at that house. There is an interesting letter from the tiresome Arthur Murphy, February 27, 1754, in which he returns his free pass to Garrick. "As I do not foresee any farther occasion for this obliging passport, I am not willing to trespass too long upon your civility," he writes. And Garrick replies: "If you choose to relinquish your right to the freedom of Drury-lane Playhouse, you will do as you please—but without the ticket, I imagine, Mr. Murphy will find the doors open to him as usual; and be it farther known to you, Sir, that as I thought you were above an undue influence, I never meant the ticket as the least tie upon the liberty of your pen or conversation."[29]

When Garrick offered the freedom of Drury Lane to General Burgoyne, author of *The Maid of the Oaks*, Burgoyne replied, November 9, 1774: "In regard to the very signal distinction you propose to me of the freedom of the house, and the manner of presenting it, I hope you will permit me to decline the parade, and at the same time believe me truly sensible of the honour of it. I should feel myself as proud to be seated in Drury-lane by your deliberate judgment of my talents, as ever an old Roman did in acquiring the freedom of *his* theatre by public services; but you are at present too partial towards me, and till I appear in my own eyes more worthy, I must request you to bound your kind intentions to an order for admittance occasionally to your Green-room, where I promise neither to criticize your men ill-naturedly, nor lead astray your ladies. The having contributed the songs and music, and other reasons alleged for my introduction to your rehearsals, will, I conclude, equally pass with the company for this additional favour, without the necessity of any farther discovery."[30]

The fact was that, as a member of society, General Burgoyne was unwilling to be recognized publicly as a theatrical author. Ordinary professional authors regarded the freedom of the house as a right, as a part of their royalties. Also on the free list, according to an 1816 Drury Lane memorandum preserved in the Enthoven Collection, were those members of the company whose salaries amounted to £3 and upwards. See also "Bones" and "Orders", pages 156, 188.

GIVING OUT THE PLAY

In the Georgian theatre even a successful piece did not obtain a complete run of consecutive performances. The programme was frequently changed, and the simple way of announcing the next day's play was to "give it out" from the stage. Pepys mentions the habit in a reference to *The English Princess*, which he saw on March 7, 1666–7: "little Mis. Davis did dance a jig after the end of the play, and then telling the next day's play."

After a first performance it was normally the new piece that was given out—an occasion always for loud partisan reactions from the audience. See page 47.

GOLD AND SILVER TICKETS

Subscription tickets to a series of plays, operas, or concerts, were often made of silver in distinction from the ordinary metal token of the theatre. Thus, Richard

Steele writes in *The Tatler*, May, 1710: "The ingenious Mr. Penkethman, the Comedian, has lately left here a Paper or Ticket, to which is affixed a small Silver Medal, which is to entitle the Bearer to see One and twenty Plays at his theatre [at Greenwich] for a Guinea." Compare with this an advertisement in *The Daily Post*, October 24, 1730: "The Silver Tickets will be ready to deliver to Subscribers at the Office in the Hay-market, on Saturday, the 31st of October, on Payment of the Subscription Money." And, in a letter from Aaron Hill to Handel, December 5, 1732: "I ought sooner to have return'd you my hearty thanks for the silver ticket. . . ."

Another kind of silver ticket was an actor's free pass in Ireland.[31] In England these tickets were made of bone. See "Bones", page 156.

Gold tickets had not the same sort of reality. A "gold ticket" was theatrical slang for a benefit ticket sold to a generous patron for a sum large enough to be reckoned in golden guineas. There is no evidence that these donations were acknowledged by any special gilt token, or gilt printed card, but some authorities are inclined to think that they were.

GREEN-ROOM

The green-room is mentioned in Shadwell's *A True Widow* (1678),[32] but to the twentieth century this place of pleasure and good company is little more than a name and a memory. Few modern theatres have such a room, and where the green-room does still exist, in a few older theatres, it is only in use on particular occasions.[33] In the Georgian theatre the green-room was the centre of theatrical society. Macklin's biography (1799) represents him as saying, with reference to an anecdote of 1735: "There were many noblemen in the green-room, full dressed, with their swords, and large wigs: (for the green-room was a sort of state-room, then, Sir)."[34] In *A General History of the Stage* (1749) Chetwood compares the green-rooms to "the most elegant Drawing Rooms of the Prime Quality"; and they seem to have been little less at the beginning of the nineteenth century, when Mrs. Mathews described them in her *Memoirs of Charles Mathews* (1838). "In the great green-room only the first class of performers was admitted, and unless in costume for any character, no-one thought of entering it except in evening dress. With regard to all ceremony and forms it resembled a private drawing-room, into which certain patrons and admirers of the drama were allowed as a privilege to enter from a door leading from the dress-boxes to the side-scenes—for there were no private boxes at that time except the manager's."[35]

A speech at the end of Act I of *Pasquin* (1736) shows that a salary qualification for the green-room existed more than a century before the date of Mrs. Mathews's book. "Sir," says the insignificant 1st Player to Trapwit, the author, "I dare not go into the Green-room; my salary is not high enough: I shall be forfeited if I go in there."

Munden's biography (1844) adds further evidence on the subject of first and second class performers. On his first engagement at Covent Garden Munden was offered £4, £5, and £6 a week, but a friend remonstrated with the manager, urging "that to render the new actor of value to the theatre, he ought to have more, at least sufficient to entitle him to the entrée of the principal green-room. The salary, it is believed, was finally fixed at £8 per week."[36]

Munden's biography also contains a picture of the green-room in 1814. "The surprising success of Mr. Kean rendered the green room of Drury Lane a fashionable place of resort. . . . The room was usually thronged, and the spectacle was rendered more attractive by the performers in character, who as they descended from their dressing rooms, advanced towards the long pier-glass at the end, examining the effect of their costume, making a grotesque or frowning face, and muttering some particular phrase, in which they judged a point could be made. During the performance Lord Byron sat in his box (the lower one on the stage, at the right hand) and raising the blind, drank his Madeira and cracked his walnuts."[37]

It was a point of green-room etiquette that certain seats belonged as of right to particular players. Tate Wilkinson perhaps makes an oblique reference to this custom (and not to a sedan chair) when describing one of Mrs. Montague's tantrums at York in 1776: "The audience called for me, and insisted on her making an apology;—however she took her chair, wished audience, manager, players, and all at the devil."[38] It is not difficult to picture the lady sitting tightly in her honoured place and refusing to budge even at the entreaty of Earby, the prompter, whose benefit performance she was deliberately wrecking.

But perhaps not: Sarah Gardner gives a similar description of herself when "Tired with such a scene of altercation, she, without disrobing herself of her theatrical habiliments, step'd into her chair and return'd home."[39]

HALF-PRICE

It was a common practice in the Georgian theatre to admit patrons after the third act at half-price. The custom was not followed in Edinburgh, Glasgow, Dublin, and Manchester, nor at Sadler's Wells, Astley's, or the Little Theatre in the Haymarket,[40] but it was the rule in most theatres, and serious riots had broken out at Drury Lane and Covent Garden when an attempt was made to suppress the privilege in 1763. Half-price was not dropped in the London theatres till the eighteen-seventies. It lingered a long time in the provinces.

The half-price system arose from a custom of the early theatre which permitted patrons to drop into the theatre free of charge after the third act. Then a small charge was made to these late-comers, and then additions were made to the programmes in order to make the second price a fair proposition.[41] Second price made sense when programmes were long and contained several items. The 1866 Leeds entertainment described under "Burletta" (see page 163) lasted three and three-quarter hours. "To prevent interruption to the performance," says the programme, "SECOND PRICE will be taken as near Nine o'clock as the end of an act, or of a play, will permit." Admission at an interval was a final refinement. In the Georgian theatre, by way of providing some additional confusion, half-price had gone by the clock. Recording a performance of *Ion* in 1836, Charles Rice remarked that Vandenhoff's "dying scene gave promise of a rich treat at the commencement, but the half-price being admitted at that moment, will plead my excuse when I say it was impossible to distinguish whether Adrastus died dumb or otherwise."[42]

HISSING

The most noticeable thing about the Georgian theatre must have been the noise. When they were indifferent the audience talked and quarrelled. When they were well pleased they applauded every notable speech, laughed, wept, and frequently collapsed in hysterics. When they were not pleased they hissed, groaned, and used cat-calls.

It is of some interest to record the variety of excuses which a Georgian audience discovered for the hideous practice of hissing. They hissed if they did not like a play: "Well, my dear Reynolds," said Kemble sardonically after a first night, "where did the hissing begin?"[43] They hissed if they detected an alteration, such as the deletion of a scene: "a great Noise, and hissing, and crying 'off, off'—the mad scene", was noted by Hopkins when the Drury Lane management decided to prune *Cymbeline*,[44] and the gallery at Norwich was properly outraged by an attempted cut of a whole act of *The Merchant of Venice*.[45] They hissed individual performers for being bad, for drying up, for being drunk, for being indiscreet. Colley Cibber was so much hissed as Scipio in *Sophonisba* that another actor took over the part at the third performance. Yates was "justly hissed", said Hopkins, because he spoke a vulgar line too audibly; it was in the text but apparently he was expected to slur it over.[46] The later Georgian audience (which was priggish as well as rowdy) would hiss a pious line for fear of condoning a profanity. "There was a slight hissing at the commencement of Bragelone's imprecation last night, occasioned by the expression 'O, Lord of Hosts'," wrote Charles Rice after a performance of *The Duchess de la Vallière* (January 7, 1837).[47]

The audience also hissed for reasons which had nothing to do with the performance. Booth was hissed for breaking his contract at Covent Garden; Kean was hissed for getting mixed up with somebody else's wife; and the lovely Mrs. Horton was hissed for taking over a part at Drury Lane which had formerly been "the property" of Mrs. Younger. Finally, political reasons were as good as any other for breaking up a performance. On March 3, 1770, Michael Kelly's play, *A Word to the Wise*, was greeted with groans and hisses merely because the author was suspected of writing for the Court party.

Sometimes the hiss was directed against members of the audience who had offended the majority. According to Fanny Burney, the Miss Cumberlands, about 1774, "were actually hissed out of the playhouse, on account of the extreme height of their feathers!"[48]

Today hissing is confined to the jocular hiss, the hiss of praise bestowed on melodramatic villains and panto-mime demons. M. Willson Disher has traced the origins of this practice to the performance of N. T. Hicks as Jonathan Wild in *Jack Sheppard* (1839). Hicks was apparently so good that the audience was carried away and joined in the execrations of the stage mob.[49]

KEEPING PLACES

Admission to the unreserved parts of many theatres was secured until quite recently (and indeed the practice probably lingers in some houses) by the purchase of a metal token at the pay box, which was handed back to the attendant at the auditorium door. This was a relic of a custom followed in the playhouse since the time of Davenant and the Restoration theatre.

M

Small metal discs were used as tickets throughout the whole period of the Georgian theatre. Bought at the pay box and surrendered in the theatre, they secured admission, but did not specify any particular seat.

In the Restoration and early Georgian theatres tickets had not been required for the box seats: the money was collected in the theatre by the box-keepers. It had been one of Garrick's early reforms to insist on tickets for the box seats also. Those who wanted good seats made early application, and it was customary for fashionable people to send their servants in advance to keep places. Indeed, it was expected of them. "To prevent mistakes" or "to prevent any disappointment", the advertisements commonly announced, "those ladies and gentlemen who have taken places are desired to send their servants by ——" Two o'clock was named at the beginning of the eighteenth century, three o'clock in the middle years, when the doors would have been opened to the public at four, and the show begun at six. Three hours was a long time to wait and naturally the ladies and gentlemen bestowed that part of the entertainment on their footmen. Later in the century five o'clock would have been early enough.

There was no such thing in the eighteenth-century theatre as a reserved and numbered ticket; but it is quite plain that those who sat in the box seats did make their own private arrangements with the box-keeper. What else can the words 'taken places' mean? Or what else can be the sense of this advertisement in *The Craftsman*, February 26, 1736–7: "Places to be had at Mr. Moor's, Box-Book-Keeper in the Play-house Passage. And Tickets to be had of Mr. Cibber at his House in Wild-Court, Lincoln's-Inn Fields." Evidently it was no use

buying a ticket for Mr. Cibber's benefit unless you also
visited Mr. Moor and arranged your *place*—a distinction
which is made crystal clear by an advertisement in
The Craftsman, March 17, 1743-4, for another Cibber
benefit. Tickets were to be bought at many addresses,
but *places* had to be obtained from Mr. Hobson at the
stage door of the theatre, and "those gentlemen and
ladies who intend to honour Mr. Cibber with their
company are desired to send their commands to Mr.
Hobson, as above; and to prevent Mistakes, they are
requested to take Tickets for the Places they order to be
kept for them."

Another explicit advertisement (Covent Garden) is one
which appeared in *The Daily Post*, December 9, 1732:
"All Persons who want Places, are desired to send to the
Stage Door (the Passage from Bow-street leading to it)
where Attendance will be given, and Places kept for the
following Nights, as usual."

Before long a reference to taking places appears in all
theatre advertisements. "Places to be had of Mr.
Hobson," and "Places for the Boxes to be taken of Mr.
Page," say the notices of Drury Lane and Covent Garden
in *The General Advertiser*, January 1749-50. Twenty-six
years later, in January 1776, *The Morning Chronicle* is
advertising "Places for the boxes to be had of Mr.
Fosbrook at the stage door," for Drury Lane; or of Mr.
Sarjant at the same place for Covent Garden. A little later
the word "(only)" is added: "Mr. Fosbrook (only)" at
Drury Lane, and "Mr. Brandon (only)" at Covent Garden
had the power to arrange the places. Next Mr. Fosbrook
and Mr. Brandon begin to conduct their business "at the
theatre", not "at the stage door". (The words "at the
theatre" had been used much earlier in the Haymarket

advertisements). And, lastly, in the nineties, the word "office" creeps into the announcements. Mr. Fosbrook is to be found at "the office, in Russel-street", Mr. Brandon at "the office, Hart-street"—and there it is, the box-office, originally an arrangement, not for the general sale of seats, but for the convenient arrangement of places in the boxes.

It is evident that this separation of booking and payment was a carefully deliberated plan, for an additional sentence which appeared in some advertisements of the sixties gives the warning: "No money to be received at the Stage Door." You had to go there for your place, but you were on no account to pay for it at the same time. It all seems unnecessarily involved and far from the practice of the twentieth century, until one remembers the irritation of buying a seat in most, though not all, theatres in Paris. You pay for your seat at one *guichet* and get it at another—which is the English eighteenth-century system in action.

The Georgian box seat, then, was reserved, and yet not reserved. There was nothing on the ticket to indicate a right to a particular seat, but plainly Mr. Fosbrook and Mr. Brandon told their clients where the seat would be, and the servant who came to keep it must have known where he had to sit or the theatre would have been the scene of daily battle. The drill is not really very mysterious. A modern parallel might be made with the business of booking a table at a big restaurant like the Savoy. You have no ticket, but you have seen the head waiter. He has made a note of where you are to sit, and, although you possess no printed evidence of the transaction, you are confident that you have only to give your name to be conducted to your place. The Georgian practice of

sending servants to keep places was an additional pre-
caution suited to a disorderly age. You had your seat,
but if you wanted to keep it, especially on a big occasion,
it was essential that you, or your representative, should
sit on it. Hence the request of the actors themselves that
"those ladies and gentlemen who have taken places"
should send their servants to see that they got them.
Keeping a seat was the customer's responsibility, not
the manager's.

Unfortunately, in that casually organized theatre, the
fashionable world could very easily obstruct itself. At
the first visit to the theatre of George III as king, "for
the first act," wrote Horace Walpole, "the press was so
great at the door, that no ladies could get to the boxes;
and only the servants appeared there, who kept places.
At the end of the second the whole mob broke in, and
seated themselves."[50] A few years later, Hopkins, the
Drury Lane prompter, noted, March 31, 1764, that the
crowd at *Othello* had been so great that it prevented
the ladies from reaching the boxes till nearly 7 o'clock.
The play began at 6.30, but, the cry being raised of "off,
off", King came forward and said that the performers
would wait. The curtain was then dropped, and the play
began again a quarter-of-an-hour later.[51]

Evidently place-keeping was an unreliable system on
important occasions, and on any occasion it was open to
objections of fraud and favouritism. "Mrs. Y sent last
week to make interest with the box-keeper, but without
success—(I suppose) by some mistake between him and
the servant," wrote Charles Yorke to Garrick, November
12, 1766.[52] And four years earlier, on November 25,
1762, a correspondent calling himself T. B. had written
a letter to Garrick on the "inconvenience arising from

the servants who are sent to keep places. I have, with concern, seen a lady finely dressed forced to sit down by a servant whose clothes and feet have been very dirty, and behaviour extremely offensive; it has happened, to my knowledge, that some servants, in order to follow their own pleasures, have hired common porters of the street to keep their places, whose company better suited a prison than a place of polite entertainment." Mr. T. B. thereupon makes the reasonable suggestion that there might be "a copper ticket marked with the letter of the box and number of the row, which tickets should be paid for upon the delivery of them to the servant who comes for places, and then the gentlemen and ladies are to carry that ticket with them as a proof of their being entitled to such a place as the number specified upon the ticket . . . which will not only prevent . . . very great inconveniences . . . but will also be a means to put a stop to that partiality from the box and book-keepers of which you possibly may be ignorant, and the method of these tickets will prevent many frauds on your part."[53]

Why did Garrick not take this sensible advice? Probably he doubted that the reserved seat would be respected without a guardian seated squarely upon it. But even if the scheme had been workable the change would almost certainly have been resisted. It had been difficult enough, earlier in the century, to induce patrons of the boxes to pay at the door. ("'Tis hoped," said a plaintive Haymarket advertisement in *The London Daily Post*, March 1736, "no Gentlemen will refuse to take a Ticket as he goes in.") In the sixties persons of fashion would probably have regarded the numbered seat as a new invasion of their liberties. Many years later Tate Wilkinson could still remark that "there is as much

jealousy as to the precedency of places with the audience
part, as there is behind the scenes for the lead of principal
characters."⁵⁴ Grand patrons enjoyed the show of sending servants to keep places. Fine ladies, says Tawdry in
Fielding's *Miss Lucy in Town* (1742), "take a stage-box,
where they let the footman sit the two first acts, to show
his livery; then they come in to show themselves, spread
their fans upon the spikes, make curtsies to their acquaintance, and then talk and laugh as loud as they are
able." They would not have liked half so well to share
an equal chance at the box-office with the general
public; they would not have tolerated an inferior person
in a superior place; and the sparkish part of the audience
would not have endured a check on their permitted
peregrinations about the auditorium. Nor, in the days of
the stock theatre, would there have been any point in
advanced booking. Patrons would not have known for
certain what they were going to see. In a leisurely world
one day was as good as another: "Ladies and Gentlemen
who have boxes for the succeeding performances of
Richard the Third, will have due notice when Mr.
Cooke will appear in that character," says an advertisement in *The Morning Post*, December 18, 1800. Lured by
the success of the new actor, the ladies and gentlemen
had booked ahead, not for a particular day, but merely
for the next time that the play happened to be performed.

The reserved and numbered ticket was a convenience
which did not make practical sense in the early or middle
Georgian theatre, and the metal tickets were still in use
at the beginning of the nineteenth century. So were the
abuses to which the system was necessarily prone.
Genest quotes an advertisement for April 2, 1810 (when
the Drury Lane company was playing at the Lyceum)

which discloses the best reason of several for the glass spy-hole still to be seen in most box doors. "Several complaints having been made to the Proprietors of the difficulty of obtaining seats without feeing the box-keepers—the frequenters of the theatre are respectfully requested to observe, that orders have been given for immediately removing the inconvenience complained of—by fixing a pane of glass in every box door; and that any Box-keeper falsely asserting that places *are taken*, or convicted of receiving money for the disposal of places not previously engaged, will be immediately discharged from the service of the theatre."

The picture reproduced opposite page 209, by Theodore Lane (1800–28), makes an important comment on this matter. Evidently there was a rule in the early nineteenth century that places, even when "taken", must be occupied by a certain hour. The custom of sending footmen had lapsed, but not the necessity of protecting one's seat.

Perhaps the officially reserved seat was established in small polite provincial theatres earlier than in London. Richard Southern draws attention in *Theatre Notebook*, vol. 1, no. 5, p. 60 (1946) to lines in *Poetical Sketches of Scarborough*, published in 1813—

> At length, all seated as they found
> Their names were ticketed around.

The affixing of names to seats is a categorical method of reservation—but it is still not the same thing as a numbered ticket, without which there can always be room for argument.

Paper tickets, usable for only one performance, were known at a very early date in the history of the theatre—

but they were chiefly used on special occasions, such as actors' benefit nights. "Both actors and authors were in the habit of soliciting their patrons' favour by personal application and by letter, and to present or enclose a printed ticket would, of course, be greatly preferable to tendering the usual brass check," remarks Montague Summers.[55] That is true, but the overruling fact was that the brass checks belonged to the theatre and were used night by night. It was not possible for the actor to dispose of the normal tickets; he was therefore obliged to provide his own, and for one performance he naturally employed the least expensive material. Early benefit tickets were often very elaborate. *The Daily Advertiser*, April 29, 1737, announces that the tickets for a Haymarket benefit will contain the prologue of the play (*The Historical Register*) "with the musick engrav'd on a copper-plate." Many of Fielding's advertisements are burlesques of advertisements, but there is no reason to suppose that this one is. The prologue (a burlesque of Colley Cibber's odes) is brief and might easily be accommodated on a ticket.

Printed tickets were not used only for benefits. In the early eighteenth century they were frequently issued when managements wanted to raise the prices or to alter the disposition of the house for some special occasion. Thus *The Daily Courant*, January 21, 1702–3 announces that at Drury Lane, "The Boxes are to be open'd into the Pit, where none are to be admitted but by printed Tickets, not exceeding four hundred in number, at Five Shillings a Ticket." At another special performance at Drury Lane, on February 10, printed tickets for a hundred seats in the front boxes were to be six shillings. This was for a "Consort of Musick" and *Marriage A-la-Mode*. Twenty-two years later a large crop of advertisements in the

Daily Courant announce performances to which "none will be admitted but by printed Tickets, which will be delivered at the Theatre." These were nearly all for programmes which included a big pantomime production —*Harlequin a Sorcerer, Apollo and Daphne, Harlequin Dr. Faustus, Jupiter and Europa*—and on many nights of the 1725–6 season (for instance) the announcement at Lincoln's Inn Fields, at Drury Lane, and occasionally at the Haymarket, ran, "None will be permitted to the Boxes but by printed Tickets": it had nothing to do with first nights—the rule was proclaimed for every occasion of acting those pieces.

The printing of these tickets is carefully noted in the daily records of Lincoln's Inn Fields. 200 or 100 is the usual number, but 600 were required for the first performance of *The Rape of Proserpine* (February 13, 1726–7). For many nights 500 tickets were printed for this piece.[56]

Lincoln's Inn Fields advertised the printed ticket much more often and for a longer time than Drury Lane did. It dropped out, except for benefits, in the thirties, after Rich had moved to Covent Garden.

The normal method of admission throughout the whole Georgian period was certainly by metal token. The printed ticket (not counting "orders", *q.v.* page 188) was not revived as a general token of admission until well into the nineteenth century. The modern fool-proof ticket, fully printed for every day of the week, was first used as late as 1884, and was invented by Charles Hawtrey.

LENGTH

"Take half a sheet of foolscap paper and divide it, the two sides are called a length by the players; and in this form their parts are always written out by the Prompter or his clerk." So runs an editorial footnote in *The Private Correspondence of David Garrick* (page 120), published in 1831–2. The manuscript contained only the lines belonging to the character, with the cues, and forty-two lines traditionally went to a length. A good early example of the word can be found in Fielding's *Pasquin* (1736), Act 1, Scene 1, where a woman player remarks that she has a part in two plays and "I wish any one else had them, for they are not seven lengths put together. I think it is very hard a woman of my standing should have a short part put upon her."

The playing of parts at short notice was so common in the Georgian theatre that an ability to learn quickly was frequently advanced as a desirable qualification in an actor. "I can repeat any part under four lengths at six hours' study", wrote Thomas Holcroft, anxious to impress Sheridan with the value of his services. "Seven or eight *lengths* were nothing to her capacity—she could *go on* for any *part* at a day's notice—valued herself on being a *quick study*"—so runs part of a satirical summary of the fascinating Miss Sally Hawk in the biography of John Edwin. Mr. Lenville, who played 'first tragedy' at the Portsmouth theatre, played parts three times as long as Thomas Holcroft's, and committed them to memory with equal despatch. "I've got a part of twelve lengths here," he told Nicholas Nickleby, "which I must be up in tomorrow night, and I haven't had time to look at it yet; I'm a confounded quick study, that's one comfort."

It is impossible to believe that an author's lines were ever very scrupulously reproduced on the Georgian stage.

An actor with a length in his hand can be seen in two of the illustrations in this book—opposite pages 32 and 33.

ORDERS

"Mr. Massingham, let the bearer have two Box Orders for this evening, if they are to be admitted. Tuesday Augt. 28th, 1810. C. Kemble."[57] Orders could only depend on the business situation at the box-office, but the writing of them was a privilege of which actors were extremely tenacious—for reasons explained by Pierce Egan in a footnote in *The Life of an Actor* (1825).[58] " 'ORDERS' to an actor, in some theatres, are almost of as much consequence, in a pecuniary point of view, as his salary. Without *orders* to accommodate their friends, performers can never make a good benefit. Persons who receive *orders* from actors are bound by a sort of *tie* to purchase tickets, when the night of the performance is announced for his advantage. We believe it was the origin of *orders*, that ultimately they should be turned to good account."

This is not a cynical statement: it is exactly confirmed in the pamphlet issued by the Covent Garden actors during the dispute of 1799–1800. "How much," they say, "the limitation of Orders must be hurtful to Benefits, is too apparent to need investigation." According to the actors, orders had been "restrained in a manner very unusual, and apparently very unreasonable," but the proprietors claimed that "orders have ever been held (and ever must be) as a gratuitous indulgence on the part of the Theatre," and Richard Hughes, the treasurer, declared: "I have never heard of any kind of pretence or claim to a right of Orders; on the contrary, they have never been allowed on any night, without special leave of the Manager,[59] and when Orders have been sent without such permission, they have been either stopped at the doors, or the amount of them deducted out of the salary of the Performer so offending against the established usage of the Theatre."

The actors replied that three of their number, on their entrance into Covent Garden Theatre, had "enjoyed the privilege of writing Orders unrestrained by any check but of their own discretion"—a "latitude enjoyed by Performers till about the year 1787, when a habit commenced . . . of charging a portion of them as cash whenever the receipts of the House should accidentally amount to a certain sum—we believe £290. As this capricious deduction from Performers' salaries depended on a casualty, there was no security from it by any human foresight." The actors, therefore, "submitted to a commutation, by which they yielded the extensive privilege handed down to them by their predecessors for the possession of a limited number of tickets (three for the boxes and four for the gallery) which being issued from the Managers, should preclude the possibility of any future mulct of this nature on the salaries." And now even the tickets were being limited.

The actors received no support in this matter from Lord Salisbury, who adjudicated the dispute. "With respect to Orders," he wrote, ". . . I think it unquestionably must be left to the Proprietors to issue them at such times, and to such extent, and on such terms, as they think proper."[60]

For many years afterwards the practice remained a matter of theatrical argument. E. Warren, inspector of checks at Drury Lane, in a letter of December 21, 1816,

described the issuing of orders as "this most troublesome
and unpleasant part of my department." At the beginning
of 1817 they were banned at Drury Lane and a note in
Warren's hand on the tally sheet for January 6 runs:
"The best House for a long time, *& not an order in the
House*. A Resolution & a wise one was passed last
Friday that all orders should be suspended." The ban
lasted a month. On February 5 a few pit orders were
allowed. During March and April the numbers slowly
mounted. On May 6 it was old times again—314 orders
in the boxes, 73 in the pit and 54 in the gallery.

An account book of Macready's management at Drury
Lane, 1841–2, shows the word "Orders" printed on
each night's return. No number is ever filled in. A number
is noted under the general heading "Free"—47 on
December 27, 1841, 81 on February 23, 1842. Presumably
this figure covered both the free privilege tickets and the
orders—the latter by this time much reduced in numbers.

Later on attempts were sometimes made to turn the
order into a money-catching arrangement. A printed
order for the Olympic, 1847, bears the legend, "Admit
the Bearer and Friends to the BOXES (on paying 1s. for
each Person) any Wednesday and Friday DURING LENT ${}^{x}_{x}{}^{x}$
This order will not be admitted unless the Parties presenting it are suitably attired."[61]

The order disappeared with benefits and low salaries
and other bad institutions of the stock theatre—but the
old slang term for free and unproductive seats still
lingers. At a time when ordinary theatre passes were
made of metal, orders were written out on paper, and
to this day "paper" is the theatrical word for a free seat.
A thin house is said to be "papered" when it has been
made to look respectable by a wide distribution of seats

usually among hospital nurses or members of Her Majesty's forces. In the modern theatre an actor may ask for seats, but he does not demand them as a natural perquisite.

PERFECT

'Perfect', meaning 'accurate', is a stage adjective of great antiquity. Costard, after his performance in "The Nine Worthies" in *Love's Labour's Lost*, says: "I hope I was perfect: I made a little fault in 'great'." Nearly two hundred years later Tate Wilkinson was writing of Dexter as "a very perfect actor in general", and the context shows that he was referring solely to Dexter's sureness on words. See "Tag", page 194. The unambiguous 'word-perfect' is more normal in this century.

PLAY-HOUSE PAY

The vague phrase "play-house pay" meant that salaries were dependent upon the number of nights that the play-house was open. Thus play-house pay indicated half-salaries during the first weeks of the season, when Drury Lane and Covent Garden only played three nights a week each; and two-thirds salaries during Lent when there were no plays on Wednesday and Friday. In Passion Week there were no plays at all and no salaries. Christmas Eve, Christmas Day, Whitsun Eve, and January 30th, the martyrdom of Charles 1st, were occasions for other deductions. It was the number of nights that the theatre was open which mattered, not the number of performances actually given by the actor. Few performers appeared every night of the week; and an actor would not have lost anything merely because the management did not choose to require his services.

But if performances were cut, salaries were cut, indeed were "liable to capricious deductions whenever Proprietors chose to shut up the House for the rehearsal of a Pantomime, or any other object of convenience to themselves;" for, as the Covent Garden actors complained in 1800, "an Actor's salary even during the season, is rated by the week, but only paid by the night." Lord Salisbury, as usual, supported the management. "The Proprietors have a right to close the theatre on such nights as they shall judge necessary for their own advantage; and the Performers' salary must cease when the theatre is closed."[62] The phrase "play-house pay" lasted a long time in the theatre. It appears, for instance, in a contract[63] signed by the manager of the Leicester Theatre in 1875, engaging William Mallalieu for £3 10s. to play "Juvenile Lead Light Comedy—with Burlesque if required."

PROMPTER

The prompter was a more important person in the Georgian theatre than the name now suggests. Sheridan said that "a stage-manager was only required for *state days* and *holidays*, but a steady prompter was the *cornerstone* of the building."[64] The prompter was an authority behind the curtain, custodian of all the parts, and all the prompt books, and consequently of all the traditions of the drama; and, with proper deference to the wishes of the leading actors, he was responsible for the staging of all the stock plays, even to the casting of the smaller parts. Witness the complaint of Holcroft to Sheridan:

"Nay, in so little esteem am I held by Mr. Hopkins, that he took the part of a dumb steward in *Love for Love* from another person, and made me do it; and when by your permission I played Mawworm, he said, had he been well and up, it should not have been so."[65] Charlotte Charke records that Simpson of Bath engaged her "to prompt, and undertake the Care of the Stage, incident to that Office".[66] See also "Understudy", page 197.

REFUSING A CHARACTER

In the stock theatre one difficulty was inescapable. It could not be easy to fit the actors to the characters. In the modern theatre an actor can refuse an engagement. In the Georgian theatre if an actor refused to play a part he necessarily precipitated a dispute with the management, which was already paying for his services. Some justice in the actors' claim to reject parts which they considered beneath their dignity was admitted by the fixing of a fine on any actor who refused his part after hearing the preliminary reading in the green-room; moreover fines were frequently remitted when the management recognized that a complaint was reasonable. The Covent Garden Treasurer, Richard Hughes, said in 1800 that Harris had not fined more than four or five people in fourteen years for refusing a character.[67] But the right to refuse was a standing nuisance and in that year the fine at Covent Garden was raised from £5 to £30. This raised a great storm among the actors, to which the management replied by pointing out that not one fine had been imposed since the new rate had been introduced. "The happy effect of it has been notorious."

N

STAR

The *Oxford English Dictionary* gives no earlier date
than 1779 for "star" in the theatrical sense. The use
must be much older than that. Colley Cibber refers to
"a blazing star" in his *Apology*, 1740.

TAG

The word "tag", meaning the last lines of a play,
has been found by Allardyce Nicoll and Sir St. Vincent
Troubridge as early as 1717, in *Three Hours After
Marriage*.

Tate Wilkinson used the word "tag" in 1790 in the
telling of an informative anecdote about an unfortunate
dry-up in *The Tender Husband*. ". . . All had gone on
smoothly till the end of the comedy, when on a
sudden even Woodward was planet struck—not one
could proceed—the audience hissed—Woodward crossed
the stage to me, and authoritatively chid me for not
speaking the tag: I said *he* was wrong, and disdained any
knowledge of a line more in my part. I spoke to Mr.
Dexter—Mr. Dexter to Mrs. Dancer (now Mrs. Craw-
ford) and with disgrace the curtain dropped: and after
each person looking on the other, like searching for
one's knee-buckle in a hurry, which at the same time is
often where it should be; so we, on inspection, found the
last speech and tag belonged to Mr. Dexter, who was a
very perfect actor in general. But the same misfortune
has been known in London to have happened: for when
it comes to the tag, as we call it, of a well-known play,
we at rehearsals, like careless people at church, begin to
move off before the blessing is pronounced; and from

that omission in the morning it begets inattention, and we fall into the pool of disgrace at night."[68]

The story is interesting because there is a superstition that it is unlucky to speak the last lines of a new production before the actual performance. Yet Wilkinson makes no reference at all to a superstition—which suggests that the custom began in laziness, that a laziness became a tradition, and that a tradition, in the course of time, attained to the venerable status of a superstition. In the Georgian theatre the tag meant a little more than merely the last lines of the play. It was that moment of sudden formality which neatly resolves everything in a moral statement, and is commonly made memorable by the use of the rhymed couplet. "Virtue, and this virtuous woman, were my first ruling passions," says old Belfield in *The Brothers*, by Richard Cumberland: and adds

> Now they resume the social soft control,
> And love and happiness possess my soul.

It is easy to understand how an actor would acquire the affectation of dismissing such lines at rehearsal with a wave of the hand—especially when the play was some familiar stock comedy which had often been rehearsed before. Tags still persisted in the Victorian theatre, where plays often ended with an arch repetition of the words of the title—but the twentieth-century drama has no tags, which accounts for the disappearance of the superstition from the modern 'legitimate' stage. All pantomimes, on the other hand, do end with a tag, and among pantomime artists the superstition is still in full flower. Principal Boys never speak the tag before the first performance.

Another reference to Tate Wilkinson and the tag comes in the reminiscences of S. W. Ryley. "I tell you what Mr. C——," he heard Wilkinson saying to one of a group of actors on the stage, "I don't like your method of tagging; when the line is formed" (i.e. the formal line of performers, traditionally ranged across the stage at the end of the play), "when all is said that can be said, and the audience are in hopes of being soon out of their misery; you pompously step forward with your poetry —or—a—be what it will, to *tag* the piece, turning your back on the rest of the performers, as much as to say 'Ladies and Gentlemen, these people behind me are but a kind of kiss-my-bottom company, I am the only object, titum, titum, titum, ti.' Pshaw sir! keep in the circle. I was in the gallery last night, and saw you come forward with 'Even Scandal dies if you approve'. I don't know whether *they* approved or not, but I'll be d——d if I did."[69]

In the early Georgian theatre it was customary to end every *act* with a tag. At that date the curtain only fell at the end of the whole play. The tag at the end of each act was a formal indication to the audience that they had reached an interval.[70]

There is a reference to forming the line for the final tag in Fielding's first play, *Love in Several Masques* (1728). Just before the last speech he has written the unnecessary stage direction, "*The* COMPANY *advance*." An old hand would not have bothered himself with such a detail. The youthful playwright was obviously delighted to show that he knew his playhouse routine. And we are the wiser for his ostentation.

UNDERSTUDY

The life of the prompter in the Georgian theatre must have been full of anxiety, for the lack of organization and the irresponsibility of the players frequently necessitated startling last minute alterations. Hopkins of Drury Lane wrote to Garrick after his retirement to describe a wonderful succession of disasters at a performance of *Much Ado About Nothing* in January, 1779. "About twelve o'clock Mr. Henderson sent word he was unable to play. We got Mr. Lewis from Covent Garden, who supplied the part of Benedick. Soon after Mr. Parsons sent word he could not play. Mr. Moody supplied the part of Dogberry; and about four in the afternoon Mr. Vernon sent word he could not play. Mr. Mattocks supplied his part of Balthazar. I thought myself very happy in getting these wide gaps so well stopped. In the middle of the first act, a message was brought me that Mr. La Mash (who was to play the part of Borachio) was not come to the House. I had nobody there that could go on for it, so I was obliged to cut his scenes in the first and second acts entirely out, and got Mr. Wrighten to go on for the remainder of the part. At length we got the play over without the audience finding it out."[71]

Four years earlier, on March 6, 1775, the play at Drury Lane had had to be changed because Reddish was unable to appear. Garrick decided on *The West Indian* (which had not been played since the beginning of the season). Mrs. Abington refused to appear. "It was not possible for her at three o'clock to read her part, get her clothes ready, and find a hair-dresser all by six o'clock, and that too at a time when she is in a very weak and ill state of health." Garrick engaged an actress "from another house" to take her place.[72]

The significant point about all these alarms and catastrophes is the fact that there were never any official understudies—although "understudy" is an old-established word in the theatrical vocabulary. "I think for fear of accidents, you should order the part to be understudied, by Mrs. Yates, as has been the general practice," wrote Murphy to Garrick, February 18, 1759. "This I mention as I find it is not done, and there is little time to lose."[73] Murphy was speaking of a new production. For one of the old stock plays the management relied upon any of the many actors who had played the parts before, whether a member of the company or a visitor from another house. Mrs. Charke writes that she applied at the *Tennis-Court* "to see (as I was universally studied) whether there was any Character wanting; a Custom very frequent among the Gentry who exhibited at that celebrated Slaughter-House of Dramatick Poetry." And sure enough it was not long before the actors were glad to call upon her services to supply the part of Captain Plume in *The Recruiting Officer*.[74]

REFERENCES

1. A sentence from an earlier play does not make quite the same distinction: "*Selfish*, this Evening, in a green Room, behind the Scenes, was beforehand with me" (*A True Widow* by Thomas Shadwell, 1678).

2. Macready, *op. cit.*, vol. 2, p. 93.

3. Planché, *op. cit.*, pp. 260-5.

4. Wilkinson, *Memoirs*, vol. 4, p. 110.

5. Davies, *Dramatic Miscellanies*, p. 184.

6. Irving, *op. cit.*, p. 531, and Augustus John *Chiaroscuro* (1952), pp. 134-5.

7. Macready objected to the receiving of presents. At his benefits he regularly returned the change when wealthy patrons sent more than the due price of their seats.

8. See *A Statement of the Differences subsisting between the Proprietors and Performers of the Theatre Royal, Covent Garden*, by Joseph Holman and seven other actors, 1800. See also Genest, vol. 7, pp. 482f.

9. See account books preserved at the British Museum of Lincoln's Inn Fields (Egerton 2265-6) and Covent Garden (Egerton 2267-2319).

10. The charge at Lincoln's Inn Fields in 1724 was £45. See accounts at the British Museum, Egerton 2265.

11. Presumably, in the context, he meant a call on his purse to meet the expenses of the house. But he could have meant another author's nightmare, the cat-call.

12. Snagg, *op. cit.*, p. 93.

13. Wilkinson, *Memoirs*, vol. 2, p. 145.

14. See Rice, *op. cit.*, p. 1. "In the hands of Miss E. Tree the character of Ion becomes so extremely effeminate that the audience cannot for an instant favour the illusion that the being before them is of the masculine gender."

15. Rosenfeld, *op. cit.*, p. 247.

16. Macready, *op. cit.*, vol. 1, pp. 32-3.

17. George Colman, *Random Records*, 1830, p. 49.

18. Planché, *op. cit.*, p. 289.

19. Wilkinson, *The Wandering Patentee*, vol. 3, p. 99.

20. Munden, *op. cit.*, p. 162.

21. Holcroft, *op. cit.*, vol. 1, p. 266.

22. Hill, *op. cit.*, vol. 2, pp. 182-3. See p. 46 above, for his letters to Garrick.

23. Reynolds, *op. cit.*, vol. 2, p. 227, note.

24. Munden, *op. cit.*, p. 98.

25. See p. 45.

26. Snagg, *op. cit.*, p. 56. And Hunt, *op. cit.*, p. 23.

27. See p. 75.

28. Boswell, *London Journal*, pp. 152-5.

29. *The Private Correspondence of David Garrick*, vol. 1, p. 66.

30. *Ibid.*, vol. II, pp. 17-18.

31. Snagg, *op. cit.*, p. 93.

32. See note 1, above.

33. An exception is the green-room in the reconstructed theatre at Stratford-on-Avon.

34. Kirkman, *op. cit.*, vol. 1, p. 140.

35. Mathews, *op. cit.*, vol. 2, p. 14.

36. Munden, op. cit., p. 32.

37. *Ibid.*, pp. 234-5.

38. Wilkinson, *The Wandering Patentee*, vol. 1, p. 222.

39. F. Grice and A. Clarke, *Theatre Notebook*, vol. 7, No. 4, p. 80.

40. See Wilkinson, *The Wandering Patentee*, vol. 2, p. 100.

41. See W. J. Lawrence, *Old Theatre Days and Ways*, p. 95.

42. Rice, *op. cit.*, p. 2.

43. Reynolds, *op. cit.*, vol. 2, p. 257.

44. MacMillan, *op. cit.*, p. 104: Feb. 6, 1764.

45. Harcourt, *op. cit.*, p. 93.

46. MacMillan, *op. cit.*, p. 97: Oct. 1, 1763.

47. Rice, *op. cit.*, p. 13.

48. D'Arblay, *op. cit.*, vol. 1, p. 52.

49. M. Willson Disher, *op. cit.*, p. 134.

50. Walpole, Nov. 24, 1760.

51. MacMillan, *op. cit.*, p. 106. Edward Everard in *Memoirs of an Unfortunate Son of Thespis*, p. 64, describes a similar scene at one of Garrick's farewell performances. Nothing of the first act could be heard and the galleries successfully demanded that the play should start again.

52. *The Private Correspondence of David Garrick*, vol. 1, p. 241.

53. Ibid., vol. 1, p. 150.

54. Wilkinson, *The Wandering Patentee*, vol. 2, pp. 179-80.

55. Montague Summers, *The Restoration Theatre*, p. 44.

56. See account books in the British Museum. Egerton, 2265-6.

57. Note in the Enthoven Collection.

58. Egan, *op. cit.*, pp. 136-7.

59. On days when orders were to be allowed a notice was posted in the green-room at noon. There is an interesting reference to orders in chapter 2 of *Nicholas Nickleby*—which is not a Crummles chapter. "The dark-complexioned men who wear large rings, and heavy watch-guards, and bushy whiskers, and who congregate under the Opera Colonnade, and about the box office in the season, between four and five in the afternoon, when they give away the orders."

60. Holman, *op. cit.*, *passim*; and Genest, vol. 7, p. 485.

61. Warren's letter, the Drury Lane tally sheet, the Macready account book and the Olympic Order are preserved in the Enthoven Collection.

62. See Holman, *op. cit.*; Genest, vol. 7, p. 485; Edward Everard *Memoirs*, pp. 202-3.

63. In the possession of the author.

64. Kelly, *op. cit.*, vol. 2, p. 41.

65. Holcroft, *op. cit.*, vol. 1, p. 266.

66. Charke, *op. cit.*, p. 195.

67. See Holman, *op. cit.*, *passim*.

68. Wilkinson, *Memoirs*, vol. 3, p. 94.

69. Ryley, *op. cit.*, vol. 3, p. 115.

70. George C. D. Odell has collected plain evidence on this point in *Shakespeare from Betterton to Irving*, 1921, vol. 1, pp. 128, 279-80, 402.

71. *The Private Correspondence of David Garrick*, vol. 2, p. 328.

72. *Ibid.*, vol. 2, p. 25.

73. *Ibid*, vol. 1, p. 99.

74. Charke, *op. cit.*, pp. 86-7.

VIII

TRADITIONS OF THE PANTOMIME

"They should, every year, have an entire *new pantomime*, or two, strongly plan'd, and enliven'd with as much *humour*, and as wanton a vein of *gaiety*, *machinery*, and *bustle*, as possible."

Aaron Hill to Barton Booth, 1732

VIII

PEOPLE who write or talk about the English pantomime usually spend a great deal of time discussing
something else—the ancient meaning of the word, the
art of mime in classical Rome, the history and development of the Italian *commedia dell' arte*. Much of this is
singularly beside the point, for though the English
pantomime has its roots in the Italian comedy, and
though the Italian Harlequin may be descended from the
Atellane farces, it is uncritical to claim stronger links,
across the darkness, with all the ancient humour of the
Saturnalia. Simple jokes are universal jokes. It is unnecessary to seek a derivation for the butter slide. This
essay approaches the subject not from the early but from
the modern end of the story. It does not look for the
jokes of ancient Rome. It attempts to discover what
remnant of our own English tradition still lingers in the
modern entertainment called pantomime.

A casual observer of this divertissement of music-hall
acts sewn together with songs and dances would certainly
suppose that it preserved very few traditions. But he
would be wrong; the pantomime has certain immortal
qualities, and the modern version would not exist at all
if it had failed to preserve them. The pantomime of
1954 may be little like the pantomime of 1854 or of 1754
and yet many things happen in it that are plainly derived
from the Harlequinade—and indeed from the *commedia
dell' arte* before it. And not only this. The pantomime in
a curious way has also become a repository for traditions

of the English stage which have died out everywhere else. We accept them in pantomime because we expect them there. It does not occur to us that we are looking at a rare survival.

The story of pantomime is like the story of a family. Your name may be Winkle. It was your father's name, and your grandfather's. The Winkles go back for two and a half centuries. But all the time they have been intermarrying with other families, and picking up their characteristics as well as maintaining the Winkle ones. You are a Winkle all right—but many of your most noticeable features are derived from the accomplished females to whom the Winkle males have surrendered over a period of many generations. Indeed, at one point, the male line died out and the name was continued only through the courtesy of an obliging gentleman, who was content to accept not only a Winkle damsel but also the Winkle name.

The English are famous for taking things from other countries, and altering them to their own uses. The pantomime, which is now so peculiarly English that it is not understood in the Dominions, and is a source of total bewilderment to citizens of the United States, was originally derived from the improvised scenes of the Italian *commedia dell' arte*—which always involved certain type characters, such as Harlequin, Pantaloon, the Doctor, and Scaramouche, were always concerned with amorous intrigues, and were normally excessively rude.

Companies of Italian actors, already extremely popular in France, had begun to visit England in the last quarter of the sixteenth century. A hundred years later, Harlequin appeared as a character in two or three Restoration plays—for instance in *The Life and Death of Doctor*

Faustus, made into a Farce with the Humours of Harlequin and Scaramouche by William Mountfort, 1697. Both appear as speaking characters, but already they exhibit the tricks, the runnings away and the trippings up afterwards familiar in the mimed harlequinade.

Early in the eighteenth century the comic figures of the *commedia dell' arte* had become so popular that many theatrical shows were followed by an entertainment of Harlequin dances, and from these, you may say, the English pantomime was evolved, chiefly through the genius of John Rich, who made his dances into a coherent story and invented that tradition of tricks and magic with which the English pantomime is essentially connected. As early as 1734 the preface to *Merlin; or The Devil of Stone-Henge* could state that "Custom . . . has made it a Sort of Necessity . . . that *Harlequin* should be a Piece of a *Magician*." Magic is still the number one tradition of pantomime.

In Rich's pantomimes a serious story was interlarded with the story of the courtship of Harlequin and Columbine. For instance, in *The Rape of Proserpine* (1727) the stage direction between Scene III (*The Gardens of Ceres*) and Scene IV (*Ceres's Palace*) reads "SCENE, *A Farm-Yard. The Grotesque Part begins.*" After Scene IV comes "SCENE, *A Country-house. The Grotesque Part continued.*" And after Scene V, "SCENE, *The Side of a Wood. The Actions of Harlequin continued.*" In the course of these interpolations, as Thomas Davies records in his *Memoirs of the Life of David Garrick*, "a variety of surprising adventures and tricks were produced by the magic wand of Harlequin; such as the sudden transformation of palaces and temples to huts and cottages, of men and women into wheel-barrows and joint-stools; of trees turned to houses; colonnades to beds of tulips; and mechanic shops into serpents and ostriches."[1]

This mixture of serious scenes and comic dances was not eccentric in a theatre which was accustomed to songs and dances, sometimes indeed comic imitations, between the acts of a tragedy. There is a curious letter of Aaron Hill's to Booth, dated December 25, 1732, advising him to prepare "little *significant* interludes of singing, dancing, and harlequinades, consisting of as many Acts, as the Play's, and succeeding them (the Acts) regularly, in short, apt sallies, so as to give the same force to your *oldest* stock Plays (which the *town* has as much, by *heart*, as the players) as if they were all, *new* and *good* ones."[2] This was fantastic, but that Aaron Hill was dimly aware of the possibilities of pantomime is shown in his next letter to Booth, in which he argues that "were the tricks of *Harlequin* connected into a *thread*, and the consequences of some story and design, they might undoubtedly, be more lively, more various, more extravagant, and surprizing. . . ."[3] He was right: pantomime could never have survived if it had not presently achieved cohesion. But even today "the grotesque part" is sandwiched between successive sections of the real story.

When the pantomime scenes were brought together to make a complete piece, the entertainment was arranged on a fixed plan. During four or five scenes, known as "the opening", a simple story was unfolded, involving the familiar quadrilateral of two lovers, the grim father, and the unwanted suitor. At the moment when the lovers were about to be separated, the good genius arrived, and turned them into Harlequin and Columbine, the father to Pantaloon, the servant to Clown. The comic characters were all underdressed and (in the later development), wore masks during this first part, so that they were ready to be transformed when the moment came. Charles Dickens has a reference to this in his description of an early nineteenth-century pantomime. "We all knew what was coming," he writes, "when the Spirit of Liberty addressed the King with the big face and His Majesty backed to the side-scenes and began untying himself behind, with his big face all on one side. Our excitement at that crisis was great and our delight unbounded." The size of these masks in the Regency and early Victorian theatre explains Dickens's repeated use of the word 'big'. They were, indeed, known as 'big heads'. That mine of Victorian information, *The Illustrated London News*, has several excellent pictures of pantomime masks, one of which (from the issue of December 29, 1849) is reproduced opposite page 224.

Then came the comic business, directed by magic and prolonged throughout a dozen scenes, in which Harlequin and Columbine were vainly pursued by the disreputable characters. Vainly, because as Fielding wrote in his pantomime burlesque, *Tumble-Down Dick* (1736), "You know, sir, or may know, that Aristotle, in his book concerning entertainments, has laid it down as a principal rule, that Harlequin is always to escape." Just before the end the lovers would be caught by the pursuer, in what was known as "the dark scene", and the magic wand would be seized by Clown—at which point the Fairy would arrive, exact from Pantaloon a promise on behalf of the young couple, and transport everyone to the final scene, which was a very grand affair indeed.

A pursuit is no longer an essential in modern pantomime. But everyone must have seen one somewhere or other. It remains a recognized tradition of the pantomime.

The scenes of the *commedia dell' arte* had words: but nothing in the English eighteenth-century pantomime— except a gag or two—was spoken. The whole thing was danced or acrobatted to music, and anything which had to be articulated was sung. Sometimes there were speaking pantomimes: but they were not the correct thing at all. The silence was partly due to a misunderstanding. The Italian actors had been forbidden to speak in Paris. What had been censorship in France was made tradition in England—a tradition which the Licensing Act was to fix as an almost unchallenged rule for as long as the original pantomime lasted.

The shape of the Georgian pantomime was faithfully preserved, decade after decade, and may be studied in many of the printed books. Here for instance is a little known early nineteenth-century pantomime, *Kelaun and Guzzarat, or Harlequin in Asia,* by J. F. Roberts, now performing, says the title page, "with unbounded applause at the Royalty Theatre." This pantomime is not recorded in the British Museum catalogue; nor does it appear in the lists in volume 2 of Allardyce Nicoll's *Early 19th Century Drama* (1930). Internal evidence shows that it was written before 1815.

The first five scenes unfold an Arabian Nights sort of story, but in spite of elaborate oriental involutions it is really the same old tale. The prince (who is Harlequin) is separated from his sultana (who is Columbine) by the machinations of Evil and a preposterous old gentleman who has invoked black art to promote the marriage of his son not to the sultana but to someone else: it is all very entangled, but you may be sure that things have gone seriously wrong, when—

13ᵈ Dec 1816   69ᵗʰ Night

The Magpie, Nota Bene, & Irishman in London

	First Account.						**Second Account.**						Orders	
	Free	Paid	Passes	£.	S.	D.	Free	Paid	Passes	£.	S.	D.	Rac	181
													W	197
Paid in Boxes		37		12	19			99		17	6	6		378
New Renter's Nominee . .	38						36						Tickets	
Subscription Nominee . . .	5						3						Ward . .	10
Free Privilege	9						10						Spring .	6
													Glwood .	2
													Byrne .	2
In Boxes.	52	37		12	19	.	49	99		17	6	6	Kelly .	2
													Dowton .	2
Passed to Boxes			2	.	7	.			8	.	12	.	Knight	2
Paid in Pit		102		17	17	.		64		6	8	.	Minden	2
New Renter's Nominee . .	18						8						Horn	4
Subscription Nominee . . .	1						5						Palmer	4
													Oxberry .	4
In Pit.	19	102		18	4	.	13	64		7	.	.	Cooke	10
													Bartley .	2
Passed to Pit			3	.	4	6			1	.	1	.	Bland	4
Passed to Boxes									1	.	2	6	Dunson .	2
Paid in Gallery		35		3	10	.		34		1	14	.	S. M. Kelly	2
														60
													Bmal	65
In 2s. Gallery.	35			3	14	6	34			1	17	6	N. Papers	66
														569
Passed to Boxes													P.t Orders	
Passed to Pit													Rac . . 102
Passed to 2s. Gallery . .			1	.	1	.			1	.	.	6	N. Papers	9
Paid Upper Gallery . . .		59		2	19	.		69		1	14	6		111
													Gallery	
													Rac 58	
													W 124	182
In Upper Gallery	59			3	.	.	69			1	15	.	Tickets .	60
														242
	71	233		37	17	6	62	266		27	19	.		
													No. Free.	
													133	

Night's Receipt . . .   65 16 6
Brought forward . . . 12752 1 .

Total . . . 12817 17 6

P. Warren

14. Taken Places Occupied. *From a coloured lithograph by Theodore Lane.*

It thunders, and all start. Hassarack and Harlequin rise from the bath, and the Genius waving her wand, they are all motionless before her, the Evil Genii trembling violently:

RECITATIVE. *Hassarack.*

Hold! tho' this Prince, awhile has felt thy pow'r,
His Genius guards him in this evil hour;
(*To Genii*) False to thy Prophet, quickly bend thy flight
To the dark regions of eternal night. (*Exit evil Genii*)
(*To Clown, etc.*) While ye weak sighted beings who dare
  pry
Into the secrets of the nether sky,
Shall bitterly repent the hour when fate
Unites Kelaun to haughty Guzzarat.

She waves her wand and everyone is transformed—one to Pantaloon, one to Clown, one to an old woman. (A direction in the previous scene notes that Yapsi is arrayed "in his caftan, with Clown's dress underneath.") Then the good Hassarack turns to the heroine.

RECITATIVE. *Hassarack.*

Tarry, sweet maid, bless'd in the constant love
Of this, your *real* Prince, you'll happy prove;
Be Columbine, (*she changes.*) You'll frolic soon with
  glee,
In the bless'd region of true liberty:
This sword will swift conduct thee to the land
Of Britain, where a firm undaunted band
Exert their courage, under freedom's sway,
And deeds of glory to the world display.

o

AIR

On the bright purple wings of delight trip
To realms of Mirth, Magic, and Joy,
To the Island, which proudly owns Liberty's sway,
Where to shake her bright throne wou'd be vain to
    essay
And where Happiness meets no alloy;
To fair England quickly flee,
The fav'rite seat of liberty
For the clime where Freedom flourishes,
Best of gen'rous passion nourishes:
Trip, skip merrily and cheerily,
Trip lightly around, with a leap and a bound
And soon you will tread on English ground.

They trip off with the Genius; and Harlequin changes scene.

Notice the antiquity of the patriotic song convention, and the easy grace with which the Fairy drags it in. In *Furibond, or Harlequin Negro*, a pantomime of much the same period, there is a particularly agreeable patriotic scene in which Britannia and a lion descend from above.

Listening to the Negro's cries,
See, Britain's Genius from the skies . . .

A fine song follows in favour of liberty.

The comic business, for which everyone has been impatiently waiting, now occupies a series of scenes, which include "A distant view of the City of Bath", "South London Water Works", "Hope Insurance Office", "Outside of a Grocer's Shop", "Farm House and Village", "Patent Shot Manufactory", "A British

Man of War on the Ocean" (another patriotic song in this one), "Cavern of the Evil Genii" (that is the "dark scene"), and "A Grand Temple". And this is the kind of thing which happened in them.

SCENE VII. South London Water Works.

Men attending, Harlequin and Columbine trip on; here Harlequin changes a water bucket, a rose tree rising from it, he plucks one while they are playing. Clown stealing on is beat off by Harlequin, and calls on the pursuers; Harlequin and Columbine doge [*sic*] Kelaun round the stage: Guzzarat continually preventing his seizure of Columbine by her caresses: Kelaun in the greatest rage, Clown in the same manner, annoying Pantaloon, till Harlequin and Columbine positively make their escape. Clown remains and examines the rose-tree, affectedly smelling it; removes it to the other trap; as he smells, a large Lizard seizes him fast by the nose; he roars out with pain, and pursuers rush on; they disengage him from the Lizard, and his nose appears of an enormous size, he still roaring with pain. Kelaun dashes off, followed by Guzzarat; Canfu fetches a Carpenter, who examines the nose, pronounces the wound mortal, unless immediately cautions [*sic*]; Clown in despair; they hold him while the Carpenter very calmly saws off his nose, the place appearing red. Clown, furious with pain, oversets them all, and pursues the Carpenter, calling "Give me my nose"; they call off much bruised, when Harlequin trips on and changes the scene.

"Harlequin changes scene" is a frequent direction. It means that the trick scenery worked as Harlequin struck with his magic bat. Benjamin Victor in his *History of the Theatres of London from the year 1760* (1771) complains that Harlequin "does nothing but run away with his Mistress and give signals with his magical wooden Sword, to direct the Men to shift the Scenes."

The next scene takes place in an Insurance Office. Clown's nose is cured by Harlequin and, in return, he promises to mislead the pursuers, who are now heard without. Harlequin hides behind a fire engine and the usual pursuit follows.

> Clown catching up the long pipe of the engine and rolling them in it, presents the brass-end to them, like a blunderbuss, when it goes off in fire-work, and, they scrumbling, Harlequin and Columbine escape; they rush after them, Clown remains and sings.

Remnants of that sort of thing will be recognized in every modern pantomime—when the ugly sisters attempt to make a pudding or the Emperor of China gets mixed up with the washing at Mrs. Twankey's laundry.

A last quotation will illustrate "the dark scene", the arrival of the Fairy, and the Grand Finale.

Things are going badly in the Cavern of the Evil Genii when Hassarack, the Good Genius, makes a fortunate appearance.

RECITATIVE. *Hassarack.*

Weak sighted wretch, who impiously arraign'd
Thy fate, which heav'n for thy good ordain'd,
Behold thy foolish wish is now complete,
And Kelaun clasps the haughty Guzzarat.

Kelaun resumes his form, Guzzarat pushes him from her, and Canfu trembles with horror.

RECITATIVE. continued.

You've met the punishment you well deserve,
Foil'd by the evil ones you wish'd to serve;
Down to the murky shades of endless night,
And learn, what heaven decrees, is right.

They sink—through traps in the stage—the scene changes, and Harlequin, Clown, and Columbine are discovered in A Grand Temple. This is the last scene, and, as in all last scenes of the pantomime, it only exists to show everyone off in a splendid setting and to facilitate the delivery of the final and essential moral.

And now, fair maid, blest by the pow'rs above,
Thus to your arms I give the youth you love:
While you, who dared oppose the evil pow'rs,
Free from their toils, shall pass your jocund hours,
And, if you still your efforts will employ,
Shall ever frolic in a round of joy.

Whereupon the courtiers enter, doubtless two by two down the great staircase in the immutable fashion of all finales, and the pantomime closes in what is opulently described as "a Grand Dance".

Pantomime reached the summit of success under the great clown Grimaldi, and began to get dull at the very moment when writers of wit were introducing new fairy tale burlesques, usually described as extravaganzas. "The burlesque extravaganzas, too, are productions increasing in popularity," wrote a theatrical critic in *The Illustrated London News* on December 28, 1844—and added the significant remark, "In fact, [at] present, the burlesque, and the introductory portion of a pantomime, are closely assimilated." "Burlesque has entirely superseded pantomime," wrote the same magazine on January 2, 1847, ". . . and we expect that the latter will, in a year or two, go out altogether, and rank with Mysteries and other dramatic productions of the past." And, gifted with the spirit of divination, it suggested that "a great hit might be made by producing a pantomime all opening." That is precisely what did happen. The burlesque squarely superimposed itself on the old beginning. It came to be the habit to play a long fairy extravaganza with a superb transformation scene at the end of it—and then to tack on to that a harlequinade which had no reference to the particular story and which got shorter and shorter with the passing of the years. A Norwich theatre bill in the possession of the author betrays the pantomime in the very act of thus changing its personality. On November 21, 1864, F. C. Burnand's *Snowdrop* had been produced at the New Royalty Theatre as an extravaganza, which is what it was. But here it is at Norwich in January, 1865, with a harlequinade stuck on at the end and the whole thing described as "Mr. W. Sidney's 11th Norwich Burlesque and Comic Pantomime".

At the beginning of the nineteenth century there was a famous production of the Arabian Nights story of *Aladdin*. No one at that time would have confused this show with a pantomime. It had no Clown or Harlequin or Columbine. It was not mimed. It was a spectacle—much as *Chu Chin Chow* was a spectacle. In the middle of

the last century there was another famous *Aladdin*—and
no one of that age would have confused that production
with pantomime either. It was an extravaganza—a
farce written in rhymed couplets. Certainly neither were
pantomimes—but both are ancestors of the thing we
now call pantomime. Much of the traditional spectacle
springs from the one, and much of the traditional
nonsense springs from the other. And notice two
significant things. In both, the part of *Aladdin* was
played by an actress—and in the extravaganza, Mr.
Henry J. Byron (on whose bones be benediction) chose
a name for Aladdin's mother that has never since been
improved upon. We owe the Widow Twankey, not to
the harlequinade but to the farcical humour of a mid-
Victorian extravaganza writer. Prince Pekoe also appeared for the first time in Byron's *Aladdin*. Twankey and
Pekoe are names connected with the tea trade—and in
that the discerning may perceive a typical Victorian jest
about China.

The next step was the introduction into the first part
of the entertainment of music-hall artists and turns—
which, although it brought into pantomime such magnificent figures as Dan Leno and Arthur Roberts, has
eventually resulted in the peculiar amalgam which passes
for pantomime nowadays, with no written book worth
notice, and everything depending on the various acts of
individual performers. During the early years of the
twentieth century, the last vestige of the old pantomime
still lingered on as the harlequinade at the tag end of the
show, but it has gone altogether now and left us with the
puzzling entertainment which inherits its ancient name,
and is apparently just as healthy as ever it was. It is not
a bit like what your great-grandfather Winkle understood

by pantomime. But, then, nor are you very like your great-grandfather Winkle. If the pantomime had gone on repeating itself for 250 years it would be as dead today as the *commedia dell' arte* is. Instead—just like the family of Winkle—it has recruited its strength from a dozen different sources—abandoning much but collecting more. The English pantomime is a very rare thing—a traditional entertainment which has kept itself young.

The harlequinade has departed. The pantomime remains—the pantomime which is no longer a pantomime, but is still full of pantomime traditions. The magic, the patriotic song, the knock-about, the interlarding of grotesque and serious, have already been mentioned. What else remains?

The old pantomime had a "dark scene", the scene before the last, where Virtue, when all seemed lost, infallibly destroyed the powers of Evil. In Rich's early pantomimes, and again in later pantomimes, it was customary to *begin* with a dark scene in which the Fairy pledged her support to some good cause or other, and a malevolent fiend expressed equal confidence in his ability to bring hero and heroine to ruin. Charles Dickens refers to "the deep gloom of the opening scene" in his preface to the *Memoirs of Grimaldi*. Nowadays it is much cut down, but in any pantomime worth calling a pantomime they still have a mysterious prologue. And when the Fairy makes her entry she will always enter from the stage right. Pantomime artists do not know anything about the history of their art, but that unchallengeable regulation is fixed even in the blondest head of hair. The Fairy Queen comes on from the stage right. And the

Demon comes on from the sinister side, from the stage left. It is a tradition as old as the miracle plays.

A story has been put about recently that the Demon comes on from the left because he was normally played by the prompter, who could thus return to his prompt corner with the least possible interruption to his principal business. This is a typical pseudo-tradition, invented by the fertile imagination of the dressing-room. The Demon may have been played by the prompter a thousand times, but the reason he comes on from the left has never been to accommodate anybody. His position is solely determined by the position of the Fairy. The right is good and the left is bad. It is essential to be clear cut about a moral issue of that sort, and so certain a rule has this always been that in most old theatres you will find the star trap in the same position, in the down stage left corner.

A star trap was a circular trap cut like the sections of half an orange. It opened at the centre from hinges on the circumference. Up would come the performer on a lift, the trap would break open and he would go flying in the air. By the time he came down again the trap had to be shut. Sometimes it did not shut, and there were ghastly accidents. I can remember seeing one used at Exeter when I was very small. What the pantomime was about I have not the smallest conception. My memory is wholly concentrated upon that extraordinary moment, when an authentic devil burst through the solid floor in a billow of rosy smoke. It is not often that a star trap is seen in action today. Few modern pantomime performers have either the skill or the courage to attempt it. Nowadays the Demon comes up through an ordinary trap, or leaps on from the wings, at which moment the Fairy, if she knows her stuff, will transfer her wand from the right hand to the left. She does this "to protect the heart", an action which undoubtedly derives directly from the harlequinade, which had a whole catalogue of traditional stances and gestures. The purpose of the movement is obvious. She wants to get the wand between her and him.

The next traditional point is that these immortal characters always speak in rhymed couplets. This convention is a very ancient one. The rhymed couplet was developed in the school of Dryden as a vehicle for high tragedy, and later by the satirists and burlesquers as a vehicle for laughter. The mid-Victorian extravaganzas, from which modern pantomime is partly descended, were entirely written in couplets—but long before them the pantomime had its own tradition of heroic verse. In the time of Grimaldi immortal characters spoke in exactly the same form and expressed exactly the same sentiments as you would hear anywhere today—witness the Fairy Hassarack's recitatives already quoted. The only difference is that the rhymed couplets were considerably better written a hundred and fifty years ago than they are today.

In a modern pantomime a few rhymed couplets are always spoken by the hero—and of all traditions of the pantomime nothing is more firmly established in the English heart than that splendid figure with her poetry and tuneful voice, her good heart and her fine leg, the principal boy.

Historians of the theatre have been needlessly mysterious about this superb phenomenon. From the moment that actresses first appeared in the English theatre they betrayed a remarkable readiness to exhibit themselves in male attire. Contemporary references are numberless. "To the Theatre", writes the excellent Samuel Pepys on October 28, 1661, ". . . where a woman acted Parthenia, and came afterwards on the stage in men's clothes, and had the best legs that ever I saw, and I was very well pleased with it." Nell Gwynn, Mrs. Reeve, Miss Santlow, Moll Davis, all appeared as men, and Mrs. Mountford, of whom Colley Cibber wrote, "While her shape permitted, she was a more adroit pretty fellow, than is usually seen upon the stage." Mrs. Bracegirdle, according to Anthony Aston, "far surmounted all the actresses of that or this age" when dressed as a man; "her gait, or walk, was free, manlike, and modest, when in breeches."

Peg Woffington was famous for her male impersonations, which included Lothario, Macheath, and Sir Harry Wildair. It was when she was playing Sir Harry that that historic retort was made, some say by Quin, others by Mrs. Clive. Peg came off the stage remarking that she believed half the audience took her for a man. "Very likely," says Mrs. Clive (I prefer to believe it was she who said it) "but do not be uneasy; the other half can convince them to the contrary."*

Mrs. Jordan played many male parts, including Sir Harry Wildair, and Lionel in *Lionel & Clarissa*. Some actresses did not limit themselves to the attractive parts. In the Hastings company in 1777 there was "a little old woman of the name of Woodward, upwards of seventy years of age who generally appeared in male characters."[4]

* Tate Wilkinson, who knew both ladies, attributes the *mot* to Mrs. Clive. So does Edward Everard in *Memoirs of an Unfortunate Son of Thespis*, 1818. W. R. Chetwood, in *A General History of the Stage*, 1749, writing much nearer the incident than either Wilkinson or Everard, gives the retort to "another Actress."

George Frederick Cooke said he had seen her in Sir Francis Gripe and The Miser, and had seen both much worse acted. Mrs. West, Mrs. Webb and Mrs. Ibbott appeared as Falstaff,[5] and in 1831 a Mrs. Hosack played Richard III at her benefit.[6] Mrs. Charke played Scrub, and was repeatedly advertised in *The London Daily Post* of 1736 to play Lord Place in *Pasquin*. Miss Edmead played Scrub, Alexander, Little Pickle, Petruchio, Captain Bobadil, and Hamlet. Many women have played Hamlet including Mrs. Inchbald, Mrs. Siddons, Sarah Bernhardt, Mrs. Bandman-Palmer, and Miss Esmé Berringer (1935).[7] Duse once contemplated playing King Lear; and a number of actresses have appeared as Romeo—Fanny Vining in 1849 at the Marylebone theatre, and Charlotte Cushman at the Haymarket in 1845 and 1855.[8] Lucille La Verne played Shylock. Madame Vestris, the greatest male impersonator of the nineteenth century, famous as Macheath and Don Giovanni, appeared so often in breeches that a waspish critic wrote of a play in which she played a woman's part, "To the shame of the age we protest that we never saw this lady perform but once before in female attire." In short, the custom was so normal, that certain parts, in whose breeches it was considered a woman would give a good account of herself, were universally known as "breeches parts", and these parts were an essential feature, first, of the Regency spectacles, and later, of the Victorian extravaganzas, from both of which the modern pantomime descends.[9]

A pedigree which includes both Mrs. Woffington and Mrs. Siddons is not likely to suggest an easy answer to the question 'who was the first principal boy?'[10] In his *Clowns and Pantomimes*, published in 1925, Mr. Willson

Disher rightly drew attention to Miss Sims, who appeared with Grimaldi in 1797 at Sadler's Wells in *Sadak and Kalasrade; or The Waters of Oblivion* by Charles Dibdin the younger. This was a pantomime with a fairy tale opening and Miss Sims appeared as one of the sons of Sadak. It does appear to have been the first example of a breeches part in a pantomime—but the point must not be over-emphasized, for *Sadak and Kalasrade* was an unusual piece, more like a spectacle than a pantomime, and Miss Sims's part was not the lead. Nor did she set a fashion; she only foreshadowed a fashion and if we are to take in foreshadowings we might equally justly return to the *commedia dell' arte* and take notice of "the first lady of the troupe, decked out like a man" who walked in the actors' parade through the streets to advertise the performance, according to Garsoni's *Piazza Universale.*[11]

The truth is that there never was a moment when a woman took over the principal boy part in a pantomime. What happened was that the pantomime was engulfed by a species of entertainment in which the principal boy was already firmly established. Miss Sims must not be forgotten, but she is not more important than Mrs. Charles Kemble (1813), Mrs. Johnston (1814), Miss Foote (1819 and 1828), Miss Stephens (1826), Mrs. Vining (1826), and Miss Vincent (1836)—all of whom played Aladdin in spectacle or opera at Drury Lane or Covent Garden. It is splitting a hair to argue that these productions were not pantomimes. The principal boy was not indigenous in pantomime; she was characteristic of a period, and an actress who appears in tights and calls herself Aladdin is a principal boy even if she appears in an oratorio.

The male impersonator was once one of the strongest traditions of the English stage. Today—except for Peter Pan, and those parts on the operatic stage which were written for women and must continue to be sung by them —the tradition is enshrined only in the splendid apparition of the principal boy.

The dame part is another last refuge of a long theatrical tradition. The coming of actresses at the Restoration did not at first prevent men actors from playing female parts, and long after the ladies had established themselves, men like Woodward, Samuel Foote and Tate Wilkinson, continued to play every kind of foolish old woman in farcical comedy. The custom was traditional also in the harlequinade. Grimaldi would appear as a comic old woman in the opening of the pantomime and then be transformed at the magic moment into Clown. In some of the earliest eighteenth-century pantomimes Harlequin disguised himself as a woman: and the joke is traditional also in the *commedia dell' arte*. Occasionally on the stage today you may see a man disguised as a woman—as in *Charley's Aunt* and many old Aldwych farces. But a man playing a woman's part is, I think, never seen.[12] It is, necessarily, the oldest of all stage traditions, but the claim of some theatrical romantics to derive the English dame chiefly from an annual frolic in ancient Rome makes very poor sense. In an age when women actors do not exist there must be female impersonators. Were there not dame parts in Aristophanes? Why all this bogus scholarship about the Saturnalia?

Occasionally a management is so misguided as to permit a woman to play the dame or one of the ugly sisters. For a woman to play dame, or for a man to play principal boy, is to attempt to make sense out of nonsense. And the queer fact is that no woman is ever as convincing as a man in a dame part. A woman puts aside her housewifely qualities when she attempts to play it. A man puts housewifely qualities on, and very often creates a positively lovable character. Look at the pictures of G. S. Melvin and Dan Leno and other great ones of the past and notice the care with which they dressed themselves. A second-rate dame always contrives to give the impression that he is what he is—a man dressed up in funny clothes. A first-rate dame deludes the imagination. She may be a very eccentric looking party. But we believe in her—because the thing that really attracts us is the personality beneath the bonnet. It is the character study, the accurate assessment of feminine foibles, that matters. You may always tell a good dame by his essential likeness, not his unlikeness, to the feminine.

Now this dame is an utterly English creation, and yet how much of the ancient spirit of buffoonery is contained in her character! There she stands, in a world of labels, schedules, permits, and restrictions, irrespressible critic of pomposity, glorious embodiment of what every free British housewife would like to be—knowing exactly how to deal with policemen, Government officials, income tax inspectors and all other nosey invaders of an Englishwoman's home. The portrait is fantastic—but always it is a reflection of truth, a commentary upon real life.

It was one of the characteristics of the original Harlequin that he was greedy. Famous *commedia dell' arte* scenes were acted in shops, and an essential part in all English pantomimes was always played by food and drink. Scenes were laid outside shops and inside shops.

Beer was drunk, fish were fried, geese were pinched, legs of mutton were brandished, stolen sausages dangled from the Clown's yawning pockets. When Grimaldi opened his mouth it was to sing about oysters, or gin. This is a tradition which has been carried straight over into modern pantomime. *Dick Whittington* always has a scene in a shop. *Cinderella*, always, and *Jack and the Beanstalk* and *Red Riding Hood*, often, have a cooking scene. *Aladdin*, which finds its main fun in the laundry, always has a scene in the market place, where you may be certain that Widow Twankey will appear on a shopping expedition. Again, nearly every pantomime, in direct imitation of Grimaldi, has a food song—about gin, or tea or tripe or rations, and as Grimaldi invited his audience to join in, so the chief comic character still does today. Jokes about food are expected. They are topical. They appeal to everyone. They are as old as the theatre.

The transformation scene, though shorn of many glories, is still to be seen in many pantomimes. This is descended both from the harlequinade and from the extravaganzas. The harlequinade transformation took a logical place in the story, for it happened when the Fairy waved her wand, rescued the characters from the gloomy caverns of "the dark scene", and despatched them to the last resplendent abode of perfection; or, as George Colman puts it in *Random Records* (1830)—when "the Guardian Genius with a wand waves and recitatives Harlequin and Columbine out of a Coal-pit, into the Temple of the Goddess of Gas."* But the transformation scene which we used to know is really more descended from

*The scene in the harlequinade when the characters were transformed to Harlequin, Pantaloon, Clown and Columbine, was known as "the Change".

15. Pantomime Masks in *Harlequin and Good Queen Bess*, Drury Lane. *From an engraving by Alfred Crowquill in "The Illustrated London News."*

16. Pantomime Scenery: Transformation scene from *Harlequin Beauty and the Beast*, Covent Garden, and a scene from the opening of *Goody Two Shoes*, Drury Lane, 1862-3. *From an engraving in "The Illustrated London News."*

the Victorian extravaganzas, which always ended with a prodigious display of gauzes and cut drops, glittering with coloured foils, and were usually described as the Realms of Delight, or the Court of Fairyland. In Burnand's extravaganza, *Snowdrop*, as advertised in a Norwich play-bill of 1865, the scene before the Harlequinade was "The Elf King's Home in the Stalactite Grotto of Prismatic Rays", and the gorgeous last scene was in "The Emerald Grove and Bower of Jewelled Flowers". When the extravaganza was tacked on to what remained of the harlequinade, the transformation scene connected the two together. Later the transformation scene was moved to the middle of the extravaganza and that is where it is usually found today, when it is found at all—at the end of the first act of the pantomime.

George Colman's reference to the Goddess of Gas is evidence of the traditional topicality of pantomime. In old pantomime books you will always find reflections upon contemporary life. Whatever the new wonder may be—insurance offices, fire engines, gas, electric light, motor-cars, aeroplanes, submarines—in they go. And, in particular, the pantomime has always been topical in the sense that it reflects with remarkable accuracy the feelings of ordinary people. Charles Dickens makes an admirable point of this in an essay in *The Uncommercial Traveller*. "I noticed," he writes, "that the people who kept the shops and who represented the passengers in the thoroughfares, and so forth, had no conventionality about them, but were unusually like the real thing— from which I infer that you may take that audience in (if you wish to) concerning Knights and Ladies, Fairies, Angels or such like, but they are not to be done as to anything in the streets. I noticed also that when two

P

young men, dressed in exact imitation of the eel-and-sausage-cravated portion of the audience, were chased by policemen and, finding themselves in danger of being caught, dropped so suddenly as to oblige the policemen to tumble over them, there was great rejoicing among the caps—as though it were a delicate reference to something they had heard of before."

The police have figured in pantomime from the time they were invented—and characters like Widow Twankey have always known precisely how to deal with them.

Certainly the modern pantomime owes a great deal to the nearest of its ancestors, the music-hall artists who have dominated the show for the last seventy years. To them it owes, in particular, the development of the dame, and those endearing characters, the brokers men—indeed all the more homely elements of pantomime as distinct from the magical or the farcical. The spirit which music hall artists have brought to pantomime is immensely important. But it must be added that although they always have a remarkable confidence in the original nature of their own performances, the truth of the matter is that the basis of all their jokes is traditional too. Breaking up the happy home? Smashing plates? Making a comic orchestra out of pots and pans? Let it be done as often as possible, but let it also be remembered that Grimaldi did the whole lot in *Mother Goose* in 1806. Sometimes one sees a dame dressed throughout in various bits of kitchen impedimenta. Aprons of dusters, ear-rings of little cake-tins, hat decorations of washing-up mops and so on. Grimaldi was making the same kind of joke when he appeared as a huzzar with a coal scuttle on each foot for top-boots.

In almost any pantomime you will see comic business

done with outsize objects—a ration book, or scissors, or beer bottles. That is one of the oldest of all pantomime traditions. Barbers were shaving people with razors like scythes in the plays of the *commedia dell' arte*. The Pope-Arbuthnot *Memoirs of Martinus Scriblerus* refers to "Harlequin trimming himself with an axe, hewing down a tree with a razor, making his tea in a cauldron, and brewing ale in a teapot, to the incredible satisfaction of the British spectator." Exaggeration in either direction is the essence of pantomime humour, and in general it prefers the large things to the little ones. It likes a feather-boa to be a feather-boa and no mistake about it.

Several comedians have made a successful turn out of speaking polysyllabic jargon with a straight and serious face. It is a good joke—but that too is descended on the one hand from Ben Jonson, and on the other from the *commedia dell' arte* character of the Doctor. And Aristophanes had the joke before them.

Some of the mechanical tricks of pantomime are said to go back to the original inventions of John Rich. The animals go back further. There were animals in the miracle plays. But in a particular sense animals have always belonged to the pantomime. They appeared in Rich's earliest creations and he himself acted a famous impersonation of a chicken. Grimaldi sang with an oyster and played games with a frog. I must confess to a deep affection for pantomime animals. Knowing, affectionate, self-willed, sublimely amoral, they transcend the normal creation. Everybody likes to see real ponies attached to Cinderella's coach—but, for the rest, we echo the remark of one Johnstone, a Drury Lane property man at the beginning of the nineteenth century. "What do I think on't?" he said, on seeing a real elephant in a

P*

pantomime at Covent Garden. "I should be very sorry if I couldn't make a much better elephant than that, at any time."[13]

Once upon a time local shops used to pay to have their names used in the shop scenes in the harlequinade. A memory even of this ancient advertising is still to be traced in pantomime. Whenever opportunity offers it is always considered the correct thing to bring in local names. It is entirely proper and eminently traditional to find that Swan and Edgar have recently opened a branch in Pekin.

The second half of the eighteenth century was particularly remarkable for its patriotic fervour and its spate of songs about jolly jack tars and the invincible might of Britannia. Sheridan nurtured the patriotic song and it has been a feature of pantomime ever since.[14] The thigh-slapper comes much later. I mean that song in which the principal boy assures everyone that good times are coming and that all that is really necessary to achieve national recovery is for everyone to smile. That dates, I think, from this century. Every pantomime ought to have a thigh-slapper—or its alternative, the marching song. The marching songs are mostly descended from the jingo songs of the Boer War period.

Processions were a cherished weakness of the Georgian theatre and that they had become an indispensible part of stage procedure is proved by Sheridan's elaborate burlesque at the end of The Critic. Processions on a stupendous scale were always a part of the Regency pantomimes, and of the pantomimes of Augustus Harris at Drury Lane in the eighteen-nineties. But they belong equally to the earliest days of Harlequin,[15] and to this day there is not a pantomime anywhere in the land which

does not end with the march-down, two by two, down
the central staircase, ending with the dazzling entry of
the Principal Boy and the Principal Girl. Tate Wilkinson
had noted that point of procedure in his *Memoirs* in 1790.
"The great personage," says he, "always appears last
in triumphal entries and processions." Stars are not
fond of yielding place. But however important the actor
may be who plays Buttons or Widow Twankey, the
great personages in a pantomime procession are always
considered to be the hero and heroine. Love conquers
all, even to a point of professional precedence.

Pantomime has transmogrified itself again and again,
while, at the same time, retaining a hundred features
picked up from different periods in the history of the
theatre. Even the names of the characters; even the
scenes, and the order in which they come, tend to become
fixed. We should be disgusted with a *Cinderella* that did
not start with a hunting chorus, and deeply shocked by a
Babes in the Wood which did not open on the village green.
You may be almost certain that the 3rd scene in any
Aladdin will take place in the laundry—which was a
pantomime scene long years before *Aladdin* was ever
put upon the stage. Scenes under the sea, which usually
occur in *Robinson Crusoe* and sometimes in *Sleeping
Beauty*, are also ancient delights, used in *Mother Goose*
in 1806, and long before that as well.

The procedure with names is interesting. Some stick.
Some don't. Dame Trot, Dame Durden, Alderman
Fitzwarren, Widow Twankey, Prince Pekoe, Prince
Charming, Dandini, are unalterable. The Baron is usually
Baron Stoneybroke, sometimes de Broke, sometimes
Hardup. The point made is usually the same—but the
name has not yet become a fixture. On him the author

may exert his fancy and on the ugly sisters. Madame Vestris appeared as King Charming in 1850, in *King Charming; or The Blue Bird of Paradise* by J. R. Planché. The more famous Prince Charming was not always called that. He has been known as Prince Primrose, and Henry J. Byron (who invented Twankey and Pekoe) called him Prince Poppetti in his *Cinderella* in 1860. Other names he took from Rossini's opera *La Cenerentola*, and accordingly the Prince's valet was called Dandini. The other Rossini names have fallen out. Dandini remains, and can thus claim one of the longest pedigrees among pantomime characters, not counting the name parts. To match with the Italian sounding names Byron included a character called Buttoni, who, soon changed to Buttons, has become one of the best loved traditional characters of the pantomime.

Pantomime today is almost as successful as ever it was. But it certainly is not good. There are three reasons for this. The first is the unlimited licence claimed by music-hall artists, who are no longer actors in the same sense that Grimaldi and Leno were actors. Grimaldi did not spend all his life in pantomime. He appeared in spectacle. He appeared in drama. He could have had a crack at anything. And within the confines of pantomime he did not always do the same thing. He was famous for his inexhaustible invention. Leno was an actor. The hurly-burly of pantomime did not prevent him from conceiving a character study. When he played a queen he was regal, even when making pastry in the royal kitchen. The modern music-hall artist is increasingly a specialist. He is famous for one particular thing. The entire performance of most of them consists in gags and quick-fire anecdotes. In itself it may be a highly accomplished

performance—but the artist never aims to create a
character other than his own. Tirelessly he strives to
project his own personality, to which end he provides
himself with a small set of catch phrases which are repeated on every occasion. The consequence is that, when
the music-hall artist appears in pantomime, he hardly acts
a part or creates a character. He wears the clothes—and
does his usual act in them. Even the catch phrases are
dragged in to make quite sure that everybody under-
stands that this is the funny man XYZ, even though he is
dressed up. Pantomime owes much to the old music-hall
artists. It owes nothing at all to those artists who regard
the pantomime stage merely as a place to repeat the acts
which they have been playing elsewhere in the summer.

The second reason for the decline of pantomime is the
elimination of the author. Time was when men like
Henry J. Byron wrote extremely amusing nonsense for
this sort of thing. Nowadays you will notice a pantomime is usually "written, devised (whatever that may
mean) and produced" by the manager himself—which is
simply to say that he has collected the gags and the
business from previous productions, and bunged in a
line or two here and there to link up the songs and the
new business contributed by the comedians: all of which
registers a great saving on author's royalties. It would
be useless for an author to write a book for a modern
commercial pantomime. The artists would not speak it
—and indeed they probably could not. Some of the
better pantomime productions are more honourable, and
make use of a good basic script, such as Hickory Wood's
Mother Goose. But it is a dangerous practice to freeze a
story into one mould. It can only lead to fossilization.

The third reason proceeds from the modern pandering

of management and artist to the alleged desires of little children. Fifty years ago children went to the pantomime at the pigtail and Eton jacket stage. They gloried in the conflict between Vice and Virtue, delighted in the powder-flashes and explosions, and awaited the outcome unafraid. Nowadays doting mothers bring their offspring to the theatre at the age of three and complain if the entertainment is above that level of understanding. The matinée auditorium is loud, not with intelligent comment (which would not matter) but with infant voices asking, "What did the funny man do that for?" "Why?" and "Can I go out?" I have known managers cut out the powder flashes for fear of frightening the little ones. I have seen the little perishers turning somersaults in the aisles from sheer boredom.

It is all an abysmal mistake—like paying dane-geld. First the excitement is lost: then the wit, for, of course, the humour must be reduced to the level of the nursery—and now even the well-loved chorus girl is being supplemented by troops of infants who are incapable of singing, dancing, acting, or even articulating, a chorus of brats on the stage for a chorus of brats in the audience. There have always been children in the pantomime—they, too, are a tradition—but it is difficult to believe that they were always as grossly inefficient or as fiercely unattractive as these. Year after year our pantomime children dance the same infantile steps and raise their tuneless voices in some arch and nauseating number. Not often do they contribute anything of charm or beauty. It was, perhaps, different in the ingenious pantomimes of the last century. In 1861, at Drury Lane, over a hundred tiny children appeared in *The House that Jack Built*, not as fatuous little dancers, but as midget labourers, engaged on the building of that famous structure—which may well have been both pretty and original.

The business is critical—but not without hope. Pantomime has always been a phœnix. It has died and resurrected again and again. In its time it has drawn refreshment from many sources—dancing and magic from one, tricks from another, spectacle from a third, rhymed couplets from one century, character creation from another. But now too many years have passed since the pantomime was last rejuvenated, and it is desperately in need of new vitality. Might not the necessary stimulus be borrowed from the 'legitimate' stage? For many years actresses have brought distinction and spirit to the principal boy. Could we not get some of the story back, performed by people who are prepared to act, not just to do an act? I hope I may not be misunderstood. Most resolutely would I oppose any arty-crafty dolling up of pantomime to make it as polite and as well-groomed as *Chu Chin Chow*. Let us be by all means vulgar. Let pastry be made, and sat on, let plates be smashed, let the crown and sceptre be mixed up with the laundry; let songs be sung of sentiment, intemperance, and inconsequence; let us have spangles and fairies on wires, and chorus girls smiling indefatigably—but for pity's sake let us have some story, some acting, some direction. If we could have those I believe we could recreate an entertainment, utterly English, which would take the roof off.

REFERENCES

1. Davies, *Garrick*, pp. 90ff.
2. Hill, *op. cit.*, vol. 1, p. 177. Hill submitted his own work to this treatment. He provided *Zara* with a set of comic interludes for use at all four intervals.
3. *Ibid.*, pp. 181-2.

4. Dunlap, *op. cit.*, vol. 1, p. 25.

5. Boaden, *Life of John Philip Kemble*, vol. 1, p. 334, and Burley, *op. cit.*, pp. 23-4.

6. Bosworth Harcourt, *op. cit.*, p. 16.

7. See also Raymond Mander and Joe Mitchenson, *Hamlet Through the Ages*, 1952, p. 24.

8. An idealized painting of 1845 suggests that Charlotte Cushman both looked and was splendid in the part; but a photograph of the 1860's (reproduced in *The Annals of the New York Stage* by G. Odell, 1931, vol. 5, p. 546) is embarrassingly coarse and ugly. It is not difficult to understand how she managed, at about the same date, to play Cardinal Wolsey.

9. See also "Breeches Parts", p. 160.

10. Some misunderstanding must have prompted A. E. Wilson in *Pantomime Pageant* to award the distinction to Miss Eglinton, who played the prince in Planché's *The Good Woman in the Wood* in 1852. Apart from the other evidence, Miss St. George, Miss Dickinson, and Madame Vestris, had all played male leads in Planché's Christmas pieces before Miss Eglinton did. Mr. Wilson gives me leave to say that he accepts this correction.

11. See Cyril W. Beaumont, *The History of Harlequin*, 1926, p. 82.

12. Roy Byford played Ursula, the pig woman, in the Phœnix Society's production of *Bartholomew Fair* in 1921.

13. There are two versions of this admirable anecdote. The above quotation is from Colman's *Random Records* (vol. 1, pp. 228-9). Michael Kelly (*Reminiscences*, vol. 2, p. 148) tells the story less well, but claims to have been present in the property room with Kemble and Sheridan when Johnstone delivered himself of the immortal dictum.

14. *Kelaun and Guzzarat* has a song about England for the Fairy, and a jolly jack tar song as well for Mr. Miller and the gentlemen of the chorus.

15. *The Heavens open, and discover* Jupiter *attended by Celestial Deities; the Earth opens, and* Pluto *and* Proserpine *rise as from Hell, attended by Infernals, at which the Followers of* Ceres *enter in a Fright.* (*The Rape of Proserpine*, 1727).

INDEX

PERSONS AND SUBJECTS

THEATRES

PLAYS